SAINTS AT THE DINNER TABLE

Saints
at the
Dinner
Table

AMY HEYD

ST. ANTHONY MESSENGER PRESS
Cincinnati, Ohio

Cover and book design by Mark Sullivan
Cover photo by Don Ventre, Ventre Photography

LIBRARY OF CONGRESS CATALOGING-IN-PUBLICATION DATA
Heyd, Amy.
Saints at the dinner table / Amy Heyd.
p. cm.
ISBN 978-0-86716-851-8 (pbk. : alk. paper) 1. Christian saints—Meditations. 2. Dinners and dining—Religious aspects—Christianity. 3. Recipes. I. Title.
BX4655.3.H49 2008
270.092'2—dc22
2008015627

Published by St. Anthony Messenger Press
28 W. Liberty St.
Cincinnati, OH 45202
www.SAMPBooks.org

Printed in the United States of America.
Printed on acid-free paper.
08 09 10 11 12 5 4 3 2 1

To my mother,

Catherine Cassidy Cahill Collins,

who not only taught me how to cook

but instilled in me my passion for it

contents

acknowledgments

Writing this book has been a wonderful spiritual journey for me. I genuinely have enjoyed delving into the lives of the saints. The encouragement and support that my family—Jim, Abby, Maggie and Charley—have shown me only has added to the experience. They tested all of the recipes that appear in this book (plus several others that did not pass their approval). I truly appreciate their honest feedback and our lively conversations about the saints.

Special thanks to Mabrouka Kuku Tiya, a fellow parishioner originally from Sudan, who showed me how to cook authentic and delicious Sudanese food. I wouldn't have been able to do justice to Josephine Bakhita without her help.

Additionally, I want to thank the staff at the Athenaeum library at St. Mary's. Their expertise and friendly help led me to fascinating information about the saints.

Thanks to my friend and editor, Mary Curran-Hackett. I treasure her friendship and extend my deepest gratitude for taking my writing and elevating it to the extent she did.

Mostly, I would like to thank both my mom and dad, who, like the saints in this book, showed me their own loving paths to holiness.

introduction

Two summers ago, after a long battle with cancer, my mother died on her birthday in her own home under the care of hospice. During that final summer I was able to spend many hours with her. (I was lucky enough to have a wonderful husband and several friends who were able to take care of my three children in my absence.) During the final month of my mother's life, I watched as parades of people came to her bedside to say a final good-bye and to thank her for the way she had touched their lives. While I have always known my mother to be special, it wasn't until this time that I became increasingly aware of the incredible impact she had on so many other lives.

My mother was a teacher for the special school district in St. Louis. She went into people's homes and taught children who were too sick to go to school. When she was dying and too ill to leave her bed, many of her former students and their parents returned the favor and came to her bedside. Because my mom was often too tired to talk, the visitors would stop to tell me firsthand how my mom made a difference in their lives. They all seemed to say the same thing: That my mother possessed a remarkable gift she could see past children's disabilities and illnesses and look right into their hearts. Time after time, she brought joy into their households. Little did they know that in my mother's and family's time of need, they would do the very same thing. Unwittingly, through their sharing of these "saintly" stories of my mother, they brought my family and me peace, comfort and, most surprisingly, joy. We all came to realize that my mother had done what Jesus asks all of us to do: "Truly, I tell you, just as you did it to one of the least of these who are members of my family, you did it to me." The more and more I thought about it, the more I realized that my mother had done all she was supposed to do, and it was indeed her time to go home to Jesus and all the angels and saints. While I realize that in all likelihood, my humble mother, a teacher for the special school district in St. Louis, won't ever formally be canonized a saint, I can't help but find comfort in the stories told to me by all her students. For in their minds, she was truly nothing less than a saint. And it is the saints to whom we turn in all aspects of our lives. It is the saints to whom we look, not just to intercede on our behalf and not just for solace and comfort, but for answers to our many questions in this earthly life.

Throughout my mother's battle with cancer, my family and I prayed to many different "official" saints. A friend told us to pray to Saint Peregrine, because he is the patron saint for cancer patients. Someone else told us to pray to Saint Catherine of Siena, because she was my mother's namesake and the patron saint of nursing. Soon I became frustrated and often lonely. I felt no connection to these saints, and, therefore, it felt as though I was praying to no one. I struggled day and night to find someone to hear my prayers and to relate to my suffering—and to my mother's. After weeks of feeling hopeless and alone, I realized that there were no MapQuest directions—no turn-by-turn instructions—that would eventually lead me to some magical revelation. Nevertheless, I kept searching.

In a moment of deep despair, I recalled a time when I had found a connection with a saint. About a year before my mom had become severely ill, it was my father who was ailing. He had a stroke and was hospitalized for about three weeks. On about the fourth day of his stay, I was very worried about his prognosis. I went roaming the floors of St. Joseph's Hospital praying—again desperately seeking answers and solace—when I walked by a statue of Saint Joseph. I looked up at him and asked, "Please, Joseph, come be with us. Please come give us strength." In that quiet and heart-wrenching moment, I felt that Joseph himself had stepped off the pedestal, took my hand and walked into my dad's room with me. I felt his presence. I felt him with my father. I received the strength I had asked and prayed for. Eventually, my dad made a full recovery and was able to be with my mom during her time of need. At the time I was somewhat surprised by my experience with Saint Joseph. I neither expected it or believed it could occur. I had been praying to saints all my life and had never felt the fullness of a response like I had at that moment.

The more I thought about it, the more I realized that Joseph had been with me my entire life. I just wasn't aware of him or, more aptly, looking for him. But the connections started to literally hit me over the head: My dad's middle name is Joseph; We were at St. Joseph's Hospital; I myself had attended St. Joseph's Academy for high school; I grew up with the teachings of the Sisters of St. Joseph. Most importantly, I had always, for reasons unknown to me, identified deeply with Joseph's own story—the dutiful servant, the caretaker, the family man, the oft-forgotten hero of the Holy Family. He was always someone I could relate to and a friend I could talk to in my time of need. I didn't have to worry that it was eleven o'clock at night. Saint Joseph was ready to listen at any time of the day.

I realize now more than ever that when I pray to a saint, I need to have some connection with that saint. I have found a wonderful listener in Saint Joseph. But I realize there are other saints out there willing to help and intercede on my behalf and to whom I can pray. In my quest to "relate" to the saints, I started an intentional journey to find a collection of saints on whom I could call. Because I am a mother of three children and enjoy cooking for my family as well as friends, I thought I would research saints that shared my interest in food and caretaking. Saint Elizabeth seemed like a good place to start because she is the patron saint of bakers and I was a finalist in the Pillsbury Bake-off contest. My middle name is also Elizabeth. Already there were small connections, but as her story unfolded, I realized she had more lessons to teach than just how to bake a really moist cake. I found a similar situation with Saint Hildegard. Thankfully, my middle name is not Hildegard, but her feast day is on my birthday. As I researched her writings about healthy cooking, I was inspired to create some healthy recipes of my own. Here were some saints that not only had some interesting commonalities with my own life, but they also had great stories to tell. Before I knew it, I was knee deep in volumes of books on all types of saints—from the likely to the unlikely—many with whom I felt deeply connected. While I was becoming spiritually inspired by each saint, each story made me think of an item of food, and eventually, I was thinking of meals I have been making my entire adult life as well as new ones I was creating that were inspired, if you will, by the saints themselves. In the end I had a treasure trove of interesting stories and recipes—meals rather. And *Saints at the Dinner Table* was born. What began as a quest to find a connection during my mother's time of need resulted in me finding my mother's soul (and all the saints she is up in heaven with) right here in my own home, my own kitchen.

While I have been transformed and inspired by many saints, I have limited this book to twelve saints whom I discuss briefly and then explain their connection to my own life and the recipes that they each inspired. In addition to Saints Elizabeth and Hildegard I have included ten other saints who speak to me in special ways. You will notice I did not include a few of the most popular or renowned "food" saints; the reason being that *foodies*, or fans of food and cooking, love to bring these saints up more for their outlandish stories than their actual connection to cooking or food. Like the martyr Saint Lawrence, for example. He is the patron saint of broiled foods. (Yes, there is a patron saint for things charbroiled!) He was awarded this distinction because, as his killers were "grilling" him by fire, in ecstasy he exclaimed that he, like a steak, was done on one side and should be turned to the other. I see the connection to food here, but the story—not so great (if anything, repulsive). Saint Christine also proved to have a colorful story and somewhat obscure connection with food. It seems that she had a seizure of some sort and everyone figured her for dead. Quickly, her family planned a Mass and burial for her. During the Mass, she awoke from her altered state. Apparently, the seizure had done something to her sense of smell, and she was repulsed by the overwhelming scent of garlic from the people attending her funeral. She could not get away from the stench fast enough, so, as legend tells us, she flew to the ceiling for escape. As you can well imagine, the mourners were terrified and fled from the church. The only two that remained were her sister and the priest. They talked her down from the ceiling, but she still had an overwhelming aversion to odors. She spent much of the rest of her life hiding in ovens and other places to escape unappealing scents. To no surprise, Saint Christine is the patron saint of psychiatrists and people with mental illness. Since I learned of her story, there have been a couple of times things were a bit crazy in my home, and I sent a prayer up to her, but I always picture her—head in the oven—not really hearing my prayer or offering me a positive alternative to my own madness. (I am sure my kids wouldn't appreciate coming home from school to find their own mom with her head in the oven!)

In addition to the unique arrangement of unlikely "cooking" saints, you will quickly discover that these recipes are varied and appeal to today's tastes rather than those of the saints' time periods. While there are some wonderful books I have discovered that prepare recipes that have a long association with a particular saint or books that show recipes that come from the saint's time period, the recipes in this book celebrate a particular aspect of each saint. I aimed to create recipes that would appeal to most people, that would not require a master's degree in culinary arts to prepare and that would entertain as well as inform. While working mostly from inspiration, I even surprised myself by the number of dishes with saintly names that seemed—at first—to not have an overt connection to a particular saint. I didn't want to leave anyone feeling frustrated or guessing where the spirit of cooking led me, so I always explain my connection between the meal and the saint before each recipe. My hope is that you feel inspired, too, and that this book serves as a friendly guidebook in your own quest to connect with—and even break bread with (as our Christian tradition calls us to do) some of our most beloved saints! Prepare the meals with your family and bring the saints alive at your dinner table.

the many ways to use this book

THE FAMILY DINNER | If you're like me, you're always trying to find new and exciting ways to connect with your family. Here is just another way to open up the lines of communication and make some fun family memories. First, pick a saint from the book and then pick a day and time that everyone can attend the meal (or if you're especially ambitious—a time that everyone can help participate in making the meal). If you have children who are old enough to read, before dinner begins ask one of them to read about the saint and present his or her story at the dinner table. You can create your own prayer or use the prayers provided at the end of each recipe to start the meal. There are also prompts for possible dinner conversation at the end of each chapter. These are merely provided to get the conversation started. Feel free to create your own questions. The idea is to share a good meal with your family and learn about a saint as well as some of the important lessons he or she has to offer. These lessons are universal and provide another way to talk to your children about being the best person each of us can be.

DINNER WITH FRIENDS (SAINT CLUB) | Dinner clubs, which are much like book clubs, are a growing trend and are a popular and fun way for friends who love to entertain and exchange cooking tips to come together. If you are one of the many people who love to exchange recipes and gather with your friends on a regular basis, you can use this book like you would any other cookbook. But instead of using different cookbooks each month, everyone in the group can take turns "hosting a saint" at the dinner table, preparing the meal and leading the discussion about the chosen saint. You can do potluck versions—where everyone can take part in preparing the meal, or you can host an entire meal yourself. Your group can determine how you would like to run the dinners.

TO FIND OUT MORE ABOUT SAINTS | It may be that you are on your own quest for saints with whom you can relate. If you are the person that does most of the food preparation in the house, you may find that many saints in this book appeal to you. This book can be used simply as a cookbook or as part of your own spiritual journey. Because the book includes one saint per chapter, you can pick it up and put it down as you have time. There is also some repetition purposefully. For example, if you haven't read about Saint Andrew yet or don't plan on cooking fish—ever— you might discover some interesting facts about him later in the book under a different saint. So many of the saints' stories overlap and in many respects, like the food they inspire, complement each other. In other words, don't feel like you have to read the book start to finish for it to make sense. Pick a recipe or a meal and start from there!

saint joseph

Patron Saint of:

Carpenters,

Happy Death,

Workers,

Fathers,

Unborn Children,

Confectioners,

Craftspeople,

Immigrants,

House Hunters,

Working People,

Cabinetmakers,

Doubters,

People With Hesitations

and

Married People

First century

Feast days:

March 19,

May 1 (Saint Joseph the Worker)

saint joseph:
father, husband, worker and protector

Together the Gospels of Matthew and Luke tell the story, albeit a brief one, of Joseph's life through the story of Jesus' infancy and childhood—and then he seems to disappear. However, despite what little information these Gospels impart, both accounts reveal Joseph to be Jesus' earthly father, protector, provider, comforter and teacher. Together the Gospels describe Joseph as a lowly carpenter and a descendant of the house of David. The stories also concur that it was during Joseph and Mary's year of engagement, or betrothal prior to marriage, that Mary became pregnant. Joseph, heartbroken, struggled over Mary's pregnancy. He knew most men of his time would have Mary stoned for such a grievous sin. But, according to the Gospel of Matthew, "an angel of the Lord appeared to him in a dream and said, 'Joseph, son of David, do not be afraid to take Mary as your wife, for the child conceived in her is from the Holy Spirit. She will bear a son, and you are to name him Jesus, for he will save his people from their sins'" (Matthew 1:20–21). Eventually, Joseph heeded the angel's announcement and took Mary as his wife, and the rest, as they say, is history.

After the famous story of Jesus' birth in Bethlehem and the presentation in the temple, Joseph had another dream warning him of Herod's intention to murder all baby boys in Bethlehem. When Joseph awoke from his dream, Matthew explains how Joseph "took the child and his mother by night, and went to Egypt, and remained there until the death of Herod" (Matthew 2:14–15). Later, Joseph had another dream, which told him it was time to return to the land of Israel. For a third time he packed up his family and their belongings and started the difficult journey back to Israel. He had planned to return to Bethlehem but realized one of Herod's more brutal sons was ruling there. Joseph made the prudent choice to settle in Nazareth. There the family was able to live the lives of typical first-century Palestinians. Their small town was only about the size of one or two large city blocks.

Joseph settled into his trade as a carpenter. While Joseph made the money, Mary took care of the household and the children. In the heat of the summer, Joseph sweat and toiled in his workshop building fine plows and furniture for his neighbors while Mary cooked, cleaned and sewed for the family. Both had difficult jobs that left them little free time. In the midst of their busy days, however, Joseph found time to teach Jesus the Torah.

Eventually, as Jesus grew older, he and Joseph probably worked side by side in Joseph's workshop. I can picture Jesus holding a newly sanded table leg ready to hand it to Joseph. As Jesus watched intently to see how Joseph fit the pieces together, I am sure Joseph took advantage of this one-on-one time with his son and capitalized on little teaching moments. Joseph, as appointed by God, was given the task to prepare Jesus for his earthly ministry. What Joseph himself could not teach, he found others to help.

When Jesus was twelve, the family went on their annual pilgrimage to Jerusalem for Passover. The family partook in all the festivities until it was time to return to Nazareth. After a day of traveling, Mary and Joseph realized Jesus was not in their travel group. Desperate to find him, they rushed back to Jerusalem. For three whole days they searched the town, until finally they went to the temple and found Jesus sitting amidst some of the greatest religious minds of the time. As the well-known story goes, after Joseph and Mary found Jesus, they were both amazed and angered. They questioned Jesus as to why he would do such a thing. Jesus responded, "Did you not know that I must be in my Father's house?" (Luke 2:49). That is the last we hear of Joseph in Luke's Gospel, and it is the first time Jesus verbalized his true connection with God. With Joseph's quiet and humble exit from Jesus' life story, he proves he had completed God's call to care for and ready the Son of Man for his ministry to the world. Again, Joseph had done what God asked of him.

REFLECTION

Life dealt Joseph an interesting hand. He married a woman already pregnant, which, I am sure, raised a few eyebrows in his day. He moved several times under difficult conditions to protect his wife and child—a child who technically was not his own, but rather, the Son of God. However, it's not that he did all these things that I find so appealing. It's his acceptance of his circumstances and fate that strikes me. While raising my three children, I try to teach them the difference between right and wrong and the importance of God in our lives. I often wonder if I am doing the best job I can or if they are even learning the important lessons. I can't imagine how I would feel if an angel came down and told me one of my children was the savior of the world. I think I would freeze into inaction—how could I possibly raise the Son of God? How and what could I possibly teach him? But Saint Joseph knew what I sometimes forget. He wasn't teaching and caring for Jesus on his own. It wasn't all on him and Mary. God was with them the entire time. Joseph's responsibility was to present the information to Jesus. God would help with the rest.

My dad was similar to Joseph in this regard. When I was a child, my dad invited me to go on walks with him. He let me direct the conversation. We talked about all of the important things in my life: ice cream, candy, a new toy. Somehow my dad could always bring the conversation around to the Gospels. He would talk about what Jesus might do or how Jesus might react. My dad just offered the idea for me to take or not. If I was ready to learn that lesson, we would get into a longer conversation about it. If I wasn't ready to learn it yet, I would start talking about something else of great importance to a ten-year-old. My dad accepted that it was his job to present the information, and he let God do the rest. I am so impatient. I want my children to learn the important lessons on my time, not theirs. That is not the way it works, not for children or for adults.

When I look at the life of Saint Joseph, I see a man who seemed to live the ideals Jesus preached during his ministry. Jesus talked about limitless compassion, love and never judging anyone. He spoke of turning the other cheek when someone hits you. When Mary hit Joseph with the ultimate blow—the child she was carrying was not his—Joseph did not seek to destroy or harm Mary. He could have had her stoned, but instead he cared for Mary and the child, as if he was his own. When Joseph woke up after his dream and immediately led Mary and Jesus to another country to keep them from danger, he placed Jesus' needs before his own. How comforting for Mary to know that her husband would do anything to keep her and her child safe.

While I was pregnant with my third child, I had many complications. I was a stay-at-home mom and was forced to go on total bed rest for fourteen weeks. The entire neighborhood seemed to pitch in to help. Three friends watched my five- and three-year-old girls during the weekdays while my husband was working at his new job. Before he left every day, he set me up with a special cooler filled with water and healthy foods. He took me to my weekly doctor's appointments. He dropped the kids off and picked them up every day. He took care of their needs and mine from the minute he got home from work until he left the next day. Even with the tremendous help that all of my neighbors provided, he had a huge load to carry. He did it all to ensure my health and the healthy birth of our third child. I hear of so many women with troubled pregnancies who don't have the support system I had. I am very lucky to have a husband who cared so much for my life and the life of our child that he continued to put us first to ensure a healthy birth. Saint Joseph was like that. When someone was in need, he immediately did everything in his power to help. He lived a normal life, but every day he made choices that made him anything but normal. He was a true man of character.

saint joseph's table (tavole di san giuseppe)

Each year the city of Sicily and many other cities across the world celebrate the feast of Saint Joseph with a special altar honoring him. Each altar is unique, but some things remain constant. Each bears a statue of the saint and is typically divided into three tiers to honor the Trinity. It is dotted with lilies to represent Joseph's purity. Various types of food are spread out over the three tiers. Typically, no meat is served as the holiday is held during Lent. The tradition started sometime during the Middle Ages after a severe drought in Sicily. The people were living under difficult famine conditions and knew they needed heavenly help to intervene. They decided to "Go to Joseph" just as people had gone to his ancestor so many centuries before (Genesis 41:55). When the farmers prayed to Joseph for help, they promised to help feed the poor with any food Joseph would help provide. When the rains came, the people rejoiced at the abundant bounty the fields produced. The citizens made good on their vow to Joseph, and each year they hold a feast on his memorial. The banquet is set, and after they give praise to God and thank Joseph for his help, they give food to the poor.

SAINT JOSEPH'S COMFORT FOOD

Inspired Menu

Saint Joseph is my favorite saint, and quite appropriately this is probably my favorite meal. It is so fitting for him. The lamb chops remind me of how Joseph helped raise Jesus, the Lamb of God. The breadcrumbs on top of the Carpenter Tomatoes resemble the sawdust that must have scattered the floors in Joseph's workshop. The mashed potatoes are a traditional comfort food and signify the comfort that Saint Joseph has always given me. The Rocky Road Cake is symbolic of the difficult roads, both literally and symbolically that Mary and Joseph had to travel during Mary's pregnancy and throughout Jesus' childhood.

SAINT JOSEPH'S GARLIC ROSEMARY LAMB CHOPS

Serves: 6

Prep time: 10 minutes

Cook time: 11 minutes

Preheat broiler to highest setting

You will need:

> 12 (5-ounce) lamb chops
>
> 3 teaspoons kosher salt
>
> freshly cracked black pepper
>
> 6 teaspoons minced garlic
>
> 6 teaspoons chopped fresh rosemary (about 3, 6-inch-long sprigs)

Sprinkle a pinch of kosher salt and a couple of grinds of cracked black pepper on one side of a lamb chop. Top this with a 1/4 teaspoon minced garlic and a 1/4 teaspoon of chopped fresh rosemary. Press this into the meat a little just to secure it. Repeat this on each side of each lamb chop. Place the lamb chops on a foil-covered jellyroll pan. (Any pan with short sides will do as long as there is space between the chops.) On the top rack of the oven, broil each side on high for 5 minutes each side to cook to medium doneness. Remove from the oven and let sit for 6 minutes before serving.

CARPENTER'S TOMATOES
Serves: 6
Prep time: 10 minutes
Cook time: 8 minutes
Preheat oven: 450° F

You will need:

> 6 Roma tomatoes, sliced
>
> 5 large leaves fresh basil, chopped
>
> 3/4 cup grated Parmesano-Reggiano cheese, divided in 1/4 and 1/2 cups
>
> 1/4 cup Italian breadcrumbs
>
> 2 tablespoons melted butter

Place sliced tomatoes in a 9 x 13-inch baking dish in a single layer. Sprinkle with fresh basil and a 1/2 cup of Parmesano-Reggiano cheese. In a medium bowl combine remaining cheese, breadcrumbs and melted butter. Sprinkle this mixture evenly over the tomatoes. Bake for 8 minutes.

GARLIC MASHED POTATOES

Serves: 6

Prep time: 10 minutes

Cook time: 20 minutes

You will need:

    6–8 medium Yukon Gold potatoes (about 3 pounds), peeled and cut into 2-inch chunks

    water to cover potatoes

    1 teaspoon salt

    1 clove garlic

    4 tablespoons butter

    3/4 teaspoon kosher salt

    1/3 cup whole milk

    pepper to taste

Boil potatoes and garlic in salted water for 15–20 minutes over medium-high heat, until the potatoes pierce easily with a fork. Drain the potatoes and add the butter, salt and milk. Mash the potatoes with a potato masher and then mix with mixer on medium for 5 minutes or until most of the lumps are gone.

ZINFANDEL GRAVY

Serves: 6

Prep time: 5 minutes

Cook time: 30 minutes

Time saver: Purchase beef gravy from the grocery store and warm it up with a sprig of rosemary.

You will need:

    1 tablespoon butter

    3/4 cup, chopped yellow onion

    3/4 cup zinfandel wine

    1 clove garlic, minced

    1 sprig fresh rosemary

    1 (14-ounce) can low-sodium beef broth

¹/₄ cup water

2 teaspoons flour

In a medium saucepan cook butter and onion over medium-high heat for 8 minutes. Stir frequently so that onions caramelize, but do not burn. Add zinfandel, garlic, rosemary and beef broth and bring to a boil. Put water and flour in a jar or a container with a lid. Shake the flour with the water until it is fully mixed. Pour the flour mixture into the boiling broth. Stir until the gravy thickens and then lower the heat to simmer until ready to serve.

SAINT JOSEPH'S ROCKY ROAD CAKE

Serves: 12

Prep time: 10 minutes

Cook time: 25 minutes

Preheat oven: 350° F

Cakes

You will need:

¹/₂ cup buttermilk

¹/₂ cup margarine (1 stick), melted

1 cup sugar

2 eggs

1 teaspoon vanilla

¹/₄ teaspoon baking soda

1 cup all-purpose flour

¹/₃ cup unsweetened cocoa powder

2¹/₂ cups mini-marshmallows

2/3 cup pecan pieces, toasted

Icing

You will need:

    5 tablespoons margarine

    3 tablespoons milk

    4 tablespoons cocoa powder

    1 teaspoon vanilla

    2 cups powdered sugar

Spray 9 x 13-inch baking dish with cooking spray. In a large bowl combine buttermilk, margarine, sugar, eggs, vanilla and baking soda. Mix on low speed for 2 minutes. Add flour and cocoa powder into liquid contents and mix for another 2 minutes. Pour batter into a greased 9 x 13-inch baking dish and bake for 20 minutes. Sprinkle mini-marshmallows over cake and bake for another 2 minutes. Sprinkle toasted pecan pieces over the marshmallows and set aside.

In a medium saucepan melt margarine with milk and cocoa powder over medium heat. Whisk constantly. When the butter is fully melted, whisk in vanilla and then the powdered sugar. Continue whisking until most of the lumps are gone. Slowly pour icing over the marshmallows and gently spread so that all of the marshmallows and pecans are covered with the icing.

DINNER CONVERSATION

Copy the following questions on pieces of paper and put them in a bowl and place on the table. While people are eating, pass the bowl around and have each person pull out a question. Everyone can take a turn answering the questions.

1. Share stories of times when someone else put your needs in front of his or hers. How did you thank that person or show gratitude?
2. Can you think of something selfless you can do for someone else?
3. If God asked you to do something difficult or even embarrassing or socially unacceptable, would you be able to say yes?
4. Would you need an angel to come talk to you in a dream to hear God's message?
5. Have you ever set aside your beliefs because it was easier or cheaper than doing the right thing?

SAINT JOSEPH'S MEAL PRAYER

Glorious Saint Joseph, model of all who are devoted to labor, obtain for me the grace to work in the spirit of penance in expiation of my many sins; to work conscientiously by placing love of duty above my inclinations; to gratefully and joyously deem it an honor to employ and to develop by labor the gifts I have received from God, to work methodically, peacefully, and in moderation and patience, without ever shrinking from it through weariness or difficulty to work; above all, with purity of intention and unselfishness, having unceasingly before my eyes death and the account I have to render of time lost, talents unused, good not done, and vain complacency in success, so baneful to the work of God. All for Jesus, all for Mary, all to imitate thee, O patriarch Saint Joseph! This shall be my motto for life and eternity.

—Pope Pius IX

notes

saint andrew
the apostle

PATRON SAINT OF:

Greece,

Russia,

Scotland,

Sailors,

Fishermen

and

Unmarried Women

FIRST CENTURY

FEAST DAY:

November 3o

andrew: the fisher of men

Like his father before him and his grandfather before that, Andrew spent his days in and around the Sea of Galilee. By the time Andrew turned six, he probably climbed over every inch of the twenty-six-foot cedar and oak boat his dad sailed. At an age when most children today start kindergarten, Andrew would have already begun to learn the family trade: fishing. I can picture little Andrew at dawn on his first day of work, sitting with his dad eating a breakfast of bread and figs. Wide-eyed, Andrew is listening to his dad talk about what the day would hold and what will be expected of him. I can even see the two walking hand in hand down to the sea and Andrew carrying empty baskets to the boat to hold their daily catch. How excited little Andrew must have been and how he must have anticipated the moment he actually got to sail out with his dad and the other men.

His jobs were simple this first day on the boat. He observed, stayed out of the way and helped put the fish into the basket. By the time the young boy grew into a strong man, he had worked every job on the boat and by the sea, and he was no longer an apprentice—he was a master fisherman. He could follow the smell of the salty fish drying out in the hot, breezy Judean air and begin the daily negotiations to sell his catch. His defined muscles could easily manage the huge nets as he cast them out into the sea. Andrew was a fisherman through and through.

Andrew fell into a daily routine. He and his brother Peter, along with James and John, worked together day in and day out to catch the fish that provided their living. One day Andrew met John the Baptist. He listened to John's message, and he recognized that John was an inspired prophet. Another time as Andrew stood with John, Jesus walked by and John exclaimed, "Look, here is the Lamb of God!" (John 1:36). Immediately, Andrew followed Jesus and spent the day listening to him. Andrew went back to his brother Simon Peter and announced, "We have found the Messiah!" (John 1:41). Andrew needed no miracle to recognize that Jesus was the Messiah, and in an instant he willingly left the only life he ever knew and loved so dearly to become a disciple of Jesus Christ.

Throughout Jesus' ministry Andrew was there as one of Christ's trusted companions and witnesses to many inspired miracles. While Andrew himself did not need Jesus to perform a miracle to convince him, Andrew recognized the power of Christ's miracles and their effects on Jesus' followers. Specifically, Andrew is mentioned in the story of the feeding of five thousand. It was Passover and the custom for the Jews to travel to Jerusalem to celebrate the great feast. Thousands of pilgrims were traveling for the celebration. Many of the people had heard of Jesus and his many miracles, and they wanted to be near him. So it happened that an enormous crowd gathered around Jesus and his apostles. Phillip remarked that "Six months' wages would not buy enough bread for each of them to get a little" (John 6:7). Then Andrew observed "There is a boy here who has five barley loaves and two fish. But what are they among so many people?" (John 6:9). Jesus instructed the apostles to seat the crowd while he gave thanks for the bread and then distributed the five loaves of bread among the five thousand people with much left to spare. This was a sign for many that Jesus was a prophet among prophets.

Andrew traveled on with Jesus providing companionship while learning and living the values Jesus preached. I wonder if Andrew realized he was beginning a new apprenticeship? How difficult it must have been for Andrew, after leaving all he had ever known and taking up and following a new trade, when his master tradesmen, his friend and confidant, was crucified. How difficult it must have been for Andrew to watch his friend and mentor die such an agonizing death. After the crucifixion Andrew must have felt empty and lost. Even though Jesus had told the apostles he would rise on the third day, they couldn't have possibly thought he would come back to life. It was on the road to Emmaus when Jesus appeared to the apostles that they recognized for certain that Jesus was not just a prophet, but the true Messiah. That had to have been the moment when Andrew realized he could not go back to his old life of fishing, but needed to spread the message Jesus preached. All of the patience and persistence Andrew learned while fishing on the Sea of Galilee prepared him for his calling. Andrew set forth as did the other apostles and began preaching the Word of the Lord.

Eventually, his travels brought him to the seaport town of Patras, Greece, where he became bishop, but he ultimately fell out of favor with the governor and was sentenced to death on a cross. His cross, however, was shaped like an X, and he was tied to it with ropes to prolong his suffering. After a long two days his agony ended, and he was reunited with Christ.

> ## *the legend of saint rule*
>
> In the fourth century Saint Rule (or Regulas) was sent by an angel to bring Saint Andrew's relics to a special location. Saint Rule set sail and didn't stop until he reached Scotland. The angel indicated he should land there and build a church around the relics. Then Saint Rule began his mission to teach the people about Jesus and Saint Andrew. He was successful and converted many people. Andrew became the patron saint of Scotland, and its flag has the white saltier (X) cross emblazoned across a blue background to honor him.

REFLECTION

Every time I hear the story of Andrew dropping his nets and following Jesus, I wonder, "How did he know it was Jesus?" I am sure I have become too cynical in my years, but if Jesus came to me today I wonder if I would recognize him? I have seen so many fallen preachers in the news that I am afraid to admit that I would most likely simply file Jesus in the same category without really giving him a chance. I have asked some of my friends this question, and they believe Andrew could feel the presence of Jesus. They believe if Jesus came back today and they were in his presence, it would be obvious who he was. Just like when he rose from the dead. He looked different on the outside, but as soon as he spoke the apostles knew they were in Jesus' presence.

I am impressed by Andrew's courage to leave everything he knew to follow Jesus. I think there are times in our lives when we receive personal invitations from God, but we choose not to follow.

One of my college roommates was always a caring person. Her personality was a wonderful mix of humor, thoughtfulness and empathy. She was a perfect fit for a career in nursing. Instead she chose to work in a high-powered job as a computer consultant for a large corporation. (We went to school in the '80s and we were all looking for the perfect yuppie job.) After a few years at the company she became pregnant and delivered a beautiful baby girl with multiple physical problems. Her daughter spent several weeks in the neonatal intensive care unit and had many surgeries before she was finally allowed to leave the hospital. For the next several months the child was in and out of the hospital until she finally died before her first birthday. The bills were astronomical and my friend spent all of her money on her daughter's medical care. With nothing left in the bank, she made the decision to quit her job and start over. She went to nursing school and is now a neonatal intensive care nurse. She is fully utilizing the talents God gave her by helping others on a daily basis. I think God had been calling her to be a nurse all along. She just couldn't take that step until she went through all she did with her daughter. Just like Andrew, it took courage for my friend to leave all that she knew and accept the call to a new life.

The story of the fishes and loaves has been told countless times. I love to imagine the looks on the pilgrims' faces when they found out that all of the food provided came from five loaves of bread and two fish. A high school teacher of mine once posed the question, "What if everyone in the crowd had brought food that day but was afraid to share it because they knew there wasn't enough for the entire audience? What if the miracle was that God inspired everyone to share?" I always loved that idea because it suggests that we can help make miracles. I think every day we are presented with opportunities to make mini-miracles. When I am standing at the checkout counter and the cashier growls something at me, I have the choice to growl back or to smile and try to say something to help him have a better day. If I can succeed at turning that one person's day around, how many other people might I affect? If I have made the cashier happy and he smiles and is nice to the rest of the people he waits on that day, in my opinion, that is a mini-miracle. God uses us as instruments to accomplish God's work. We just have to listen to God as Andrew listened to Jesus.

SAINT ANDREW'S FISHER OF MEN MEAL

Inspired Menu

This meal of salmon with maple soy glaze, baked sweet potato with cinnamon and honey and asparagus salutes Andrew's life as a fisherman and a "fisher of men." Although salmon is not a fish Andrew would have eaten, it is popular, tasty and easy to find at most grocery stores. The Saint Peter's Staffs (asparagus) recognize Andrew's brother, who was with him throughout his travels with Jesus. The fig cake for dessert incorporates figs and dates that are so plentiful near the Sea of Galilee.

SAINT ANDREW'S SALMON WITH MAPLE SOY GLAZE

Serves: 6

Prep time: 5 minutes

Cook time: 15 minutes

Preheat oven: 400° F

You will need:

    2½ to 3 pounds salmon fillets

    1½ cups pure maple syrup

    1 cup low-sodium soy sauce

    3 tablespoons Dijon mustard

    3 teaspoons chili garlic sauce (found in the Asian section of the supermarket)

Place salmon fillets skin side down in a 9x13-inch glass baking dish. In a separate bowl mix maple syrup, soy sauce, Dijon mustard and chili garlic sauce. Pour this marinade over the salmon. Bake in oven for 10–15 minutes. The thicker the salmon, the longer it will take to bake. The salmon will be ready when it flakes easily and looks opaque in the center.

ANDREW'S "SWEET LIFE" BAKED SWEET POTATOES WITH CINNAMON AND HONEY

Serves: 6

Prep time: 5 minutes

Cook time: 50 minutes

Preheat oven: 400° F

You will need:

    6 medium size sweet potatoes

    6 tablespoons honey

    cinnamon to taste

Wash sweet potatoes, and prick three or four times with a fork. Place in oven and for 40–50 minutes. The potatoes will be ready when you can easily pierce them with a fork. Remove from the oven and cut in half lengthwise. Sprinkle with cinnamon then drizzle each sweet potato with about 1 tablespoon honey.

SAINT PETER'S STAFFS
Serves: 6
Prep time: 10 minutes
Cook time: 10 minutes
Preheat oven: 500° F

You will need:

18 asparagus spears, cleaned and stems removed

9 paper-thin slices proscuitto

3 tablespoons butter, melted

1/8 teaspoon garlic salt

1/8 teaspoon dried oregano

1/2 teaspoon lemon zest

3 tablespoons shredded Parmesano-Reggiano cheese

Wrap each asparagus spear with a half slice of proscuitto and then place into a 2-quart baking dish. In a medium bowl mix melted butter, garlic salt, oregano and lemon zest. Pour the butter mixture over the asparagus. Bake the asparagus for 7–10 minutes. The asparagus should be cooked but somewhat crisp. Remove from the oven and sprinkle with Parmesano-Reggiano cheese before serving.

GALILEE FIG CAKE
Yields two 9-inch cakes (12–14 servings)
Prep time: 30 minutes
Cook time: 30 minutes
Preheat oven: 350° F

Note: The cake can be baked a day ahead of time. If two cakes are too much for your gathering, wrap one in foil and plastic wrap and freeze for up to two months.

Cakes
You will need:

1 (9-ounce) package of dried mission figs, stems removed

3/4 cup water

1/4 cup sugar

3/4 teaspoon ground cinnamon

 3/4 cup canola oil

 1 cup sugar

 1 teaspoon vanilla

 3 large eggs

 1/2 cup buttermilk

 1 3/4 cups all-purpose flour

 1 1/2 teaspoons baking powder

 1/2 teaspoon salt

 1/2 teaspoon baking soda

 1 (5.1-ounce) box instant vanilla pudding mix

 2 teaspoons cinnamon

 1 large Granny Smith apple, skinned and chopped

Topping

You will need:

 1/2 cup brown sugar

 1/2 cup all-purpose flour

 1/2 cup quick oats

 1/2 cup chopped pecans

 4 tablespoons melted butter (about half of a stick)

Place figs, water, sugar and cinnamon in a large, covered saucepan and bring to a boil for 5 minutes. Remove from heat and set aside to cool for at least 10 minutes. Place in a food processor. Pulse the figs for 10 seconds until a chunky sauce forms.

In a large bowl combine oil, sugar, vanilla, eggs and buttermilk with a mixer on low for 2 minutes. In a separate bowl sift together flour, baking powder, salt, baking soda, vanilla pudding mix and cinnamon. Gradually mix the dry ingredients into the wet. Pour the fig mixture into the batter and stir to combine. Stir in chopped apple.

Pour the batter into 2 greased 9-inch cake pans.

Pour the brown sugar, flour and oats into a large bowl and stir to combine. Add the nuts and butter and stir with a fork until a crumbly topping forms. Sprinkle this on top of the cakes.

Bake for 40–45 minutes. Cover the cakes with foil for the last 20 minutes of baking to avoid burning. Let the cakes sit for 10 minutes before removing them from the pans.

DINNER CONVERSATION

Copy the following questions on pieces of paper and put them in a bowl and place on the table. While people are eating, pass the bowl around and have each person pull out a question. Everyone can take a turn answering the questions.

1. Do you think you could recognize Jesus if he came today? Would you be open to hearing his Word?
2. Describe an opportunity you had to make a mini-miracle.
3. Do you think you are doing what God is calling you to do?
4. Do you think you could have lived the life of an apostle?
5. If you were Andrew, would you be able to "drop your nets and follow Jesus"?

SAINT ANDREW'S MEAL PRAYER
Christ Has No Body

Christ has no body but yours,
No hands but yours,
No feet but yours.

Yours are the eyes through which
Christ's compassion must look out on the world.

Yours are the feet with which
He is to go about doing good.

Yours are the hands with which
He is to bless us now.[1]

—Attributed to Saint Teresa of Avila

NOTE
[1] The Roundtable Association of Diocesan Social Action Directors, *Living God's Justice: Reflections and Prayers* (Cincinnati: St. Anthony Messenger, 2006), p. 132.

notes

saint martha

PATRON SAINT OF:

Cooks,

Dieticians,

Innkeepers

and

Servants

FIRST CENTURY

FEAST DAY:

July 29

saint martha: the reluctant hostess

Now as they went on their way, he entered a certain village, where a woman named Martha welcomed him into her home. She had a sister named Mary, who sat at the Lord's feet and listened to what he was saying. But Martha was distracted by her many tasks; so she came to him and asked, "Lord do you not care that my sister has left me to do all the work by myself? Tell her then to help me." But the Lord answered her, "Martha, Martha, you are worried and distracted by many things; there is need of only one thing. Mary has chosen the better part, which will not be taken away from her." (Luke 10:38–42)

A typical day for a first-century woman living in Bethany, like Saint Martha, was a difficult one, filled with grueling work. In order to make a single loaf of bread, Martha had to start her day before dawn to trek to the granary to purchase grain. After the long walk there and back home again, Martha ground the grain into coarse flour. This task alone required patience, strength and stamina. The repetitive motion of turning the stones made her arms burn in pain. Once the grain was ready, Martha added the remaining ingredients and prepared the dough. Already sore from grinding the grain into flour, Martha then began the process of kneading the dough into a ball. Then in the heat of midday (around 90° Fahrenheit), Martha prepared a fire outside to bake the bread.

Once she was done tending to the bread over the hot fire, she moved to her garden to gather the ingredients to assemble the rest of the meal. After she finished compiling all of the ingredients, which could take up to two hours, she would again have to walk, probably several miles, to the well to acquire the water for boiling. How her shoulders must have ached from carrying those buckets day after day. Without giving her muscles a rest, she would begin the task of making dinner. But this is a typical day—imagine what Martha's day would have been like if she knew

Jesus, the Son of God, was coming to dinner! It couldn't be just any meal, and the house couldn't look just OK. Everything would have to be perfect! In addition to preparing the meal, she would have to pour fresh oils and perfumes throughout the home. She would have so much to do to prepare without a moment to rest! No wonder she was so grumpy by the time Jesus arrived at her house!

Her frustration is understandable. And she probably felt a little bit embarrassed to be scolded by Jesus. Instead of getting mad at Jesus and fighting her position, she looked inward and heard Jesus' message. *Don't worry that someone else might be getting something more. Worry about you, Martha. Focus on what you need to be doing, not what you think someone else should be doing.* If Martha had closed her mind to what Jesus was trying to tell her, she never could have believed with that certainty that Jesus was the Messiah. After her grueling day and embarrassment of being scolded, she internalized his message and tried to become a better person.

REFLECTION

I can really empathize with Saint Martha. She had to be feeling very proud of herself. She, an ordinary woman, was preparing dinner for the Son of God. Then her sister, Mary, sits down and starts listening to Jesus. Suddenly, Martha stops concentrating on the wonderful honor she has been given, and her focus shifts to this perceived injustice. Martha has to do all of the work while her sister, Mary, gets to relax and listen to Jesus.

How many times have I been preparing dinner and had similar thoughts? There I am in my own happy world cooking and then I look out the window and see my husband playing basketball with the kids. Suddenly, my focus shifts, and I start ruminating about why he gets to be out playing and having all of the fun while I am inside doing all of the work. He gets playtime, and I get housework time. "I want some playtime, too," I huff.

It is easy to get caught up in worrying about what someone else is getting. When I stop worrying about my perceived injustices and focus on the gains I have, my life is remarkably more pleasant. Martha was so open to Jesus' message that she learned this quickly. I love how human she was. She had some of the same feelings of resentment we all have occasionally. Yet she listened, processed the message and internalized it. It is not so much when I am cooking that I think of Martha, but when I feel slighted and can't quite let go that I pray to her for help. She understands those feelings and can help rid me of them.

martha and the dragon

According to legend, Martha, Mary and Lazarus moved to Tarascon, France, in between Arles and Avignon, several years after the death of Jesus. Apparently, there was a terrible dragon that lived in a nearby lake. The brave warriors in the villages went to fight the dragon only to be maimed or killed. The village was living in fear, and no one knew how to stop the beast. One day one of the villagers approached Martha. They knew of her stories about Jesus and his miracles and they felt maybe she could help. Martha traversed through the woods and found the dragon next to the lake eating the remains of the last warrior that approached him. Quickly, Martha sprinkled holy water over the beast and held up her crucifix. The holy items immediately hypnotized the dragon, and the villagers charged the dragon and pelted it with arrows. The town was overjoyed at the dragon's death. To this day there is a festival called Jeux de la Tarasque held at the end of June in Tarascon that celebrates this occasion.

Saint Martha's Gimme-A-Break Meal

Inspired Menu

The meal below is one that allows you to be Martha and Mary at the same time. It is designed to be both a nutritious and fun dinner for the entire family to enjoy. The pizza and sundae bars are a wonderful way to get your kids involved in the meal preparation. Most children enjoy having the choices for their pizzas and sundaes as well as the assembly line.

Saint Martha's No Worries Pizza

Serves: 6–8

Prep time: 1½ hours (including rising time)

Cook time: 15–30 minutes, depending on oven space

Preheat oven: 500° F

Pizza Dough

You will need:

    2 tablespoons active dry yeast (2 packages)

    1¾ cups warm water (110° F to 115° F)

    ¼ teaspoon sugar

    1½ teaspoons salt

    3 tablespoons honey

    3 tablespoons warm milk

    1½ tablespoons olive oil

    5–6 cups all-purpose flour

    1 teaspoon olive oil

    5 tablespoons melted butter

    ¼ teaspoon garlic salt

In a large bowl dissolve the yeast into the warm water. Add the sugar and stir well. Let the yeast proof for about 5 to 10 minutes until it looks foamy. Add the salt, honey, milk and oil and stir briefly. Add the flour 1 cup at a time until it forms a ball. Keep adding flour until the dough is only slightly sticky. You may not need to use all the flour. On a well-floured surface knead the dough for 5 minutes. Place a teaspoon of olive oil in a large bowl. Place the dough into the bowl and move the dough around until it and the bowl are covered with oil. Place a warm, wet dish towel over the bowl of dough to cover. Set aside for an hour so the dough will rise to double its size.

    After the dough has risen, remove it from the bowl and knead it for 1–2 minutes. Cut the dough into 6 to 8 equal parts. Roll each dough segment into a 7- to 8-inch round. Place the rounds on greased baking sheets.

    Mix the garlic salt into the melted butter and brush this onto the pizza crusts and then lightly on the rest of the dough.

Possible Toppings

precooked crumbled Italian
    sausage

thinly sliced red onion

pepperoni

thinly sliced fresh green
    peppers

Canadian bacon

sliced fresh mushrooms

crumbled bacon

sliced tomatoes

black olives

roasted garlic

feta cheese

goat cheese

shredded mozzarella

fresh mozzarella slices

grated Parmesan cheese

(You are limited only to your imagination here. Think of your favorite toppings at a restaurant. Provide the ingredients that work for your family.)

Pizza Sauce

You will need:

    1 (15-ounce) can crushed tomatoes

    2 tablespoons tomato paste

    1 teaspoon olive oil

    1/2 teaspoon dried oregano flakes

    1/4 teaspoon garlic salt

    1 tablespoon honey

Stir in all ingredients in a medium saucepan and cook over medium heat for 10 minutes. The sauce can be prepared ahead and stored in the refrigerator.

Place the pizza sauce into its own bowl and set it next to the pizza dough rounds. Place all of the ingredients into separate small bowls and line them up after the cheese, or place the ingredients in separate piles on a large serving platter. Place a large bowl of the shredded mozzarella at the end of all the ingredients. Once you have set up the assembly line, bring the family in and create your own pizzas together. The pizzas work best if you begin with the sauce, then add your ingredients and top it off with cheese.

Bake the pizzas for 10–15 minutes until the cheese begins to bubble.

Time saver! Substitute already made pizza sauce instead of making your own. There are various quick alternatives for the dough as well. Premade crusts can be found near the pizza sauce at the supermarket. Refrigerated dough in a tube can be found where the refrigerated cookie dough is located. Lastly, frozen bread dough makes a nice crust as well. This requires some forethought as you need to thaw the dough. The convenience items come in handy when you want to spend some family time preparing the pizza, but don't have the time to do all of the prep work of actually making the dough and sauce yourself.

saint andrew: patron saint of fishermen pizza

Bake an 8-inch pizza dough covered with garlic butter in a 500°F oven for 6 minutes. Place 5 medium shrimp and some lump claw crab meat from a can onto the baked dough. Add a couple of roasted garlic cloves. Top with mozzarella cheese. For a finishing touch, sprinkle with dried oregano and some hot red pepper flakes. Place the pizza in a 500° F oven for 5 minutes until the cheese is bubbly.

MARY'S LAID-BACK MIXED GREENS WITH BALSAMIC DRESSING

Serves: 6

Prep time: 10 minutes

Salad

You will need:

  1 (6-ounce) bag prewashed mixed spring greens

  1/2 cup grape tomatoes sliced in half

  1/2 cup cucumber cut into 1/2-inch slices, then quartered

  1/4 cup blue cheese crumbles

Place the greens, tomatoes, cucumbers and blue cheese crumbles into a large salad bowl. When ready to serve, pour balsamic dressing over the greens to your taste. Mix the salad.

Balsamic Dressing

You will need:

  5 tablespoons olive oil

  2 tablespoons balsamic vinegar

  1 tablespoon Dijon mustard

  1 teaspoon minced garlic

  2 teaspoons granulated sugar

Place all of the ingredients into a jar or container with a lid. Shake the dressing until it is emulsified. This can be stored in the refrigerator for up to 2 weeks. You will need to reshake the dressing before pouring it onto the greens.

Saint Martha's Everybody-Helps-Themselves Sundae Bar
Serves: 6–10
Prep time: 15 minutes

Sundae Bar
You will need:

 ¹/₂ gallon vanilla ice cream

 1 jar caramel sauce

 1 jar chocolate fudge

 1 jar raspberry sauce

 6 Oreo cookies, crumbled

 1 (1.55-ounce) Hershey chocolate bar, chopped

 1 (1.5- ounce) Reese's peanut butter cups, chopped

 1 (3.7-ounce) Snickers bar, chopped

 1 (2.1-ounce) Butterfinger bar, chopped

 1 (1.69-ounce) bag M&Ms

The sundae bar is set up much like the pizza construction zone. Again, the toppings I have listed here are just suggestions. You may prefer gummy worms and circus peanuts on your sundaes.

Scoop 1–2 scoops of vanilla ice cream into a bowl. Repeat until there is a bowl for each person. Set the bowls at the head of the bar. Place the sauces next. (These typically taste even better when they are warmed up a little in the microwave first.) Next, place each topping into its own individual bowl and set next to the sauces.

Each person is now ready to create his or her own sundae!

saint ambrose sundae

Saint Ambrose is the patron saint of beekeepers. He was awarded this distinction because legend tells us that a swarm of bees landed on his mouth when he was a baby. He is often depicted with a swarm of bees or near a beehive. Some say the bees foretold his great oratory abilities. Mix the following ingredients for a bee-liciously inspired sundae.

Servings: 1
Prep time: 5 minutes

2 scoops vanilla ice cream
2 tablespoons warmed honey
1–2 tablespoons of your favorite dark chocolate, chopped into pieces
2 tablespoons chopped honey-roasted cashews

DINNER CONVERSATION

Copy the following questions on pieces of paper and put them in a bowl and place on the table. While people are eating, pass the bowl around and have each person pull out a question. Everyone can take a turn answering the questions.

1. Can you think of times in your life when you feel like Martha?
2. What can you do to help find the joy in the thing you are doing when you really want to be doing something else?
3. How do you think Martha felt when Jesus scolded her?
4. How would you have reacted if you were Martha?
5. When you are feeling resentment toward someone, what can you do to let it go?

SAINT MARTHA'S MEAL PRAYER

Psalm 23 for Busy People

The Lord is my pace-setter, I shall not rush;

he makes me stop and rest for quiet intervals,

he provides me with images of stillness,

which restore my serenity.

He leads me in the way of efficiency,

through calmness of mind;

and his guidance is peace.

Even though I have a great many things to accomplish each day

I will not fret, for his presence is here.

His timelessness, his all-importance will keep me in balance.

He prepares refreshment and renewal

in the midst of activity,

by anointing my mind with his oils of tranquility;

my cup of joyous energy overflows.

Surely harmony and effectiveness shall be the fruits of my hours

and I shall walk in the pace of my Lord,

and dwell in his house for ever.[1]

—Toki Miyashina

NOTE

[1]Veronica Zundel, *Eerdmans' Book of Famous Prayers* (Grand Rapids, Mich.: William B. Eerdman, 1983), pp. 114–115.

notes

saint brigid
of ireland

PATRON SAINT OF:

Dairy Workers,

Brewers

and

Ireland

Born: circa 450

Died: circa 525

FEAST DAY:

February 1

brigid: ireland's bridge to christianity

Saint Brigid's life story is a tough one to tell. Not because it's tragic or sad, but because so much of her life is literally a mystery—a hodgepodge, really, of historical hearsay and straight-up pagan Celtic folklore. And with an approximate fifteen hundred year span since her death, it seems there is more legend than historical fact left to tell. However, most historians agree on the facts of Brigid's birth: She was the daughter of a pagan chieftain of noble birth. Her mother was a Christian slave, who was sold away from her father's household soon after her birth. Then the story becomes the subject of debate. (In other words, you will find various stories about Brigid's life after the point of her birth that differ greatly.)

Most historians believe that Brigid was raised by a druid, but she must have been able to see both her mother and father occasionally, because many stories speak of Brigid's influence on her father, and many tell of her mother's influence on her. In fact, Brigid must have learned about Jesus from her mother because at a young age Brigid began to practice Christianity, namely through acts of charity and love for others. One story tells of a time when Brigid found her father beating a servant, and she mustered up the courage to stand up to her father and beg him not to strike the servant with one more lash. Thanks to her intercession, her father stopped beating the servant.

Other stories tell of Brigid's chastity, despite many suitors who pursued her and despite the fact that she was incredibly beautiful. One story says that her father had even planned for her to marry a bard, but Brigid declined the offer and told him that she was "called" by God to be a nun. At sixteen she rejected marriage and took the vows of poverty, chastity and obedience to become a nun.

What we lack in facts between her birth and her entrance into the abbey, we make up for in her power and influence over Ireland as a nun. Eventually, Brigid became the first abbess of a convent. Throughout her life as a nun, which is documented, she traveled throughout Ireland opening new convents. In Kildare Brigid ran an abbey that housed both nuns and brothers (each had their own respective wing, of course). The men were able to provide the priestly help the nuns desired, as well as the muscle for the hard labor required to maintain a large abbey. The nuns did the cooking and cleaning and traveled through the town providing help to those who needed it. Brigid's charity continued throughout her life, and this was evident in how she ran the abbey. The doors of the convent were always open to those in need. Travelers passing through always received a warm meal and a comfortable place to stay. Under Brigid's leadership the abbey in Kildare became one of the largest in Ireland.

Many, however, still confuse Saint Brigid with the Celtic fertility goddess, also named Brigid. For centuries the Celtic people followed a pagan religion much like Greek or Roman mythology. Their main god, Daghdha, fathered a fire-headed goddess named Brigid.[1] The poets continually sang praises of her beauty and enumerated her powers over light, fire, healing, wisdom and literature. Year after year the Celtic people held a festival called *Imbolc* on February 1 in her honor. The fete (or festival) celebrated the emergence of the new light of springtime. The culmination of the festival was the sacrificial slaughtering of a ewe to coax the goddess into granting a prolific spring.[2] One such festival was held near a sacred oak tree. For years pagan virgins kept a fire burning by this tree in honor of the goddess.

Although we in the Catholic church don't celebrate pagan Celtic folklore, it is nevertheless interesting to see how much of Saint Brigid's life and legend overlap with Brigid the goddess. When Saint Brigid built her abbey in Kildare, it was on the site of this sacred oak tree. In fact, the word *Kildare* means "church of the oak tree." The virginal nuns kept the fire lit. Each night a different nun kept watch to make sure the fire wasn't extinguished. When Brigid died, the nineteen remaining nuns continued the tradition. On the twentieth night one of the sisters would look to the heavens and say, "Brigid, tend that fire of thine, for this is thy night." The fire stayed lit for over a thousand years.[3] Another legend that linked the two Brigids described fire emanating from Saint Brigid's childhood bedside all the way up to heaven. From early times fire was a symbol for the deity. It was natural for the Celtic people to confer the powers of their fire goddess onto their new Christian leader.

One favorite legend of the *saint* Brigid states that she was present during the birth of Jesus Christ. One day a white dove gently fluttered past Brigid, catching her attention. Focusing only on the bird, she followed it until she found herself in the midst of Jesus' birth. She acted as midwife for Mary and assisted in Jesus' birth, and blessed him with water to unite him with the earth. The animals around the stable weren't able to give milk until Brigid sang a lilting melody to urge the milk to flow. Other legends portray the saint Brigid performing miracles resembling those Jesus performed in the Gospels. As a young child Brigid helped milk cows, churn butter and make cheese. Some poor people in the village came asking for any food she could spare. It wasn't Brigid's food to give, but she couldn't let the people go hungry. She gave away all of her father's dairy products. Fearing a lashing from him, she prayed to God that the food would be replenished. Just like when Jesus dispensed the fishes and loaves near the Sea of Galilee, the food increased enough to feed everyone and more than replenish what was eaten. On another occasion, when Brigid was the abbess at Kildare, some visiting priests came to stay at the abbey. Saint Brigid didn't have any ale to offer her guests, so she turned some dirty bathwater into sweet ale for the priests.

Saint Brigid's life, in many ways, formed a "bridge" that many people were able to pass over from their rich ancestry and history with Celtic paganism to their future in Irish Christianity. Whenever the Celtic people came into contact with Brigid, they must have noticed her acts of charity and care for others and her worship of this strange foreigner, Jesus of Israel. It was most likely an exciting experience for them to be in the presence of someone who was so close to God. Soon, people all across the counties of Ireland came to know and love her. As time passed, legends, truths and the stories of the pagan goddess Brigid became part of Saint Brigid's own legacy. As all of the stories intertwined into one full vision of Saint Brigid, pagans began to hear and understand the story of God and Jesus Christ.

saint brigid's cross

Throughout Ireland one will see crosses made of rushes hanging over the doors of various houses. The tradition started years ago when Saint Brigid was at the house of a dying pagan chieftain. She sat with the man to help him through his pain. While she was next to him, she began to tell him the story of Jesus Christ. While she talked, she gathered rushes from the floor and carefully weaved them together into the shape of a cross. As she finished describing Jesus' passion, she also finished the cross and presented it to the chieftain as a reminder of Jesus. Upon hearing this new message of salvation, the chieftain began to renounce his pagan ways and turned to Jesus Christ. The dying man was miraculously healed, and he, too, began to spread the word of Jesus Christ.

REFLECTION

I think sometimes people need to put a face on an issue in order to understand and become more aware of it. There are several examples in which issues have been brought to the forefront once a celebrity attached his name to a cause. A lot of people weren't aware of the suffering going on in Darfur, Sudan, until George Clooney directed an episode of *ER* highlighting the issue. Many people had never considered having a colonoscopy until Katie Couric's husband died of colon cancer, and she had one on air in order to create awareness about colon cancer and to encourage screening. When we first started hearing about the AIDS virus in the early 1980s, people were so afraid of catching the deadly disease that they shunned those infected with it. Elizabeth Taylor, along with some other key celebrities, took on the cause and now not only are there some fantastic drugs available to combat the disease, the afflicted are no longer treated like lepers.

It is not always a celebrity making an impact. I remember a commercial that aired when I was a child. It showed polluted air and streams with dying fish. The commercial ended by showing an American Indian with a tear running down his cheek. I know there is still a long way to go, but since that commercial aired we have made significant strides toward educating people on the importance of reducing pollution in this country and around the globe. Many times our lives get so busy that we don't see what's going on around us. Unfortunately, sometimes it takes something or someone we can relate to before we will listen to new ideas. When Saint Brigid assumed some of the attributes of the goddess Brigid, she became a familiar face the pagans could listen to. Her Christian-pagan legends helped the people of Ireland accept Jesus Christ into their lives.

SAINT BRIGID'S IRISH FEAST

Inspired Menu

Inspired by some of Ireland's traditional ingredients—fish, potatoes and cabbage—I set out to make a meal that not only used these ingredients, but put a twist on what we have come to know as Irish fare—corned beef and cabbage, shepherd's pie and fish and chips. Because Saint Brigid is the patron saint of dairy workers, I instead wanted to infuse lots of dairy products—cream and butter—in three of the four dishes. (These meals are not for the faint of heart—literally!)

SAINT BRIGID'S SALMON WITH GINGER CITRUS CREAM SAUCE

Salmon

Serves: 6

Prep time: 2 minutes

Cook time: 15–20 minutes

Preheat oven: 400° F

You will need:

    1 (2 to 2¹/2-pound) salmon fillet

    1 cup milk

    salt to taste

    pepper to taste

Place the salmon skin side down in a 9 x 13-inch glass baking dish. Pour the milk around the sides of the salmon. Sprinkle the salmon with salt and pepper to taste. Bake for 10 to 15 minutes. The thicker the salmon, the longer it will take to cook. The salmon will be opaque and flake easily when it is ready.

GINGER CITRUS CREAM SAUCE

Serves: 6

Prep time: 5 minutes

Cook time: 10 minutes

You will need:

    1 shallot finely chopped (about 3 tablespoons)

    1 small clove garlic, minced (about ¹/4 teaspoon)

    1 tablespoon butter

    ¹/2 teaspoon salt

    1 teaspoon all-purpose flour

    1 tablespoon fresh lime juice

    2 tablespoons orange juice

    1¹/2 tablespoons grated fresh ginger

    1 cup cream

    1 tablespoon chopped cilantro

Place shallots, garlic and butter in a 2-quart saucepan over medium heat. Cook for 3–4 minutes until the shallots soften. Stir to prevent the garlic from burning. Add the salt and flour and turn heat to low. Stir constantly while cooking for another 2 minutes. Stir in lime juice, orange juice and ginger until an emulsion forms. (This will only take about a minute.) Stir in cream and then add cilantro.

COLCANNON

Serves: 6

Prep time: 20 minutes

Cook time: 15 minutes

Time saver: Use store-bought refrigerated mashed potatoes and heat fully. Mix in some arugula and green onions for a quick version of colcannon.

You will need:

2½ pounds russet potatoes, skinned and chopped into 2-inch pieces

water to cover potatoes

1 teaspoon salt

4 tablespoons unsalted butter

¾ cup whole milk

½ teaspoon salt

dash freshly ground black pepper

1½ cups chopped arugula

4 green onions, finely chopped

Place the chopped potatoes in a 3-quart pot and cover with water. Add the salt to the water and cook over medium heat for 12–15 minutes. The potatoes will be ready when they are easily pierced with a fork. Drain the pot of all water. Cut up the butter and add it to the potatoes. Using a fork or potato masher, begin to mash the potatoes. Add the milk and continue mashing. Sprinkle the salt and pepper and mash some more. When the potatoes are mostly lump free, add the arugula and green onions.

Serve immediately. Alternatively, you can prepare ahead of time and store in the refrigerator. To reheat, add a couple of tablespoons of milk to the potatoes, cover with plastic wrap and warm in the microwave.

BRIGID'S COLD CABBAGE SALAD
Serves: 6–8
Prep time: 15 minutes

Salad

1 (16-ounce) package coleslaw cabbage

1/2 cup green serrano pepper julienne cut into 1-inch x 1/8-inch strips

1/3 cup red bell pepper julienne cut into 1-inch x 1/8-inch strips

1/2 cup snow peas julienne cut into 1-inch x 1/8-inch strips

1/4 cup green onions, sliced diagonally

1/2 cup skinned orange, cut into 1/4-inch thick wedges

In a large salad bowl mix the cabbage, serrano pepper, bell pepper, snow peas, green onion and orange. Cover this and leave in the refrigerator until 10 minutes before you are ready to serve.

Dressing

2 tablespoons lime juice

6 tablespoons olive oil

1/2 teaspoon grated fresh ginger

1 tablespoon sugar

1 crushed beef bouillon cube

salt

pepper

Place the lime juice, olive oil, ginger, sugar, bouillon cube, salt and pepper into a jar or container and cover with lid. Shake up all of the ingredients to combine. Place into the refrigerator until 10 minutes before you are ready to serve. Pour the dressing over the slaw. Use salad tongs to toss the dressing into the slaw.

BRIGID'S CHOCOLATE ORANGE CHEESECAKE BARS

Serves: 9

Prep time: 15 minutes

Cook time: 35 minutes

Preheat oven: 350° F

You will need:

    36 Oreos

    3 tablespoons melted butter

    2 (8-ounce) packages low-fat cream cheese, softened (Neufchâtel cheese)

    1 cup granulated sugar

    2 eggs

    2 teaspoons pure vanilla extract

    finely grated zest from 1 orange (about 2 teaspoons)

Pulse 30 cookies in a food processor for 2 minutes until the cookies have turned into a crumbly mixture. Add the melted butter and pulse for 10 more seconds until the butter is fully mixed in. Pour the cookie crumb mixture into the bottom of a greased 2-quart baking dish and press it down with your hands to form a crust. Set this aside. Pulse the remaining 6 Oreos and set aside for garnishment.

Using a mixer on medium, mix cream cheese and sugar until smooth. Add the eggs, vanilla and orange zest. Spread the cream cheese mixture over the chocolate crust. Sprinkle cookie crumbles evenly over the cheesecake mixture.

Bake for 30–35 minutes or until cake looks a little bit higher in the center than on the sides and is a golden brown.

Remove from the oven and slide a knife around the sides of the pan and then slice into squares. Chill in the refrigerator for at least 4 hours before serving. Store leftovers in the refrigerator.

DINNER CONVERSATION

Copy the following questions on pieces of paper and put them in a bowl and place on the table. While people are eating, pass the bowl around and have each person pull out a question. Everyone can take a turn answering the questions.

1. What must it have been like for a pagan to hear the story of Jesus and realize there is only one God?

2. Why do you think the nuns kept the fire burning all of those years?

3. Consider the legend of Brigid present at Jesus' birth. What message was that supposed to present to believers and nonbelievers alike?

4. Can you think of a time when you were made aware of an issue through a celebrity? What issue was it and who put a "face" on the issue for you?

5. Do you think the pagans would have accepted Christianity as quickly without the help of Saint Brigid?

SAINT BRIGID'S KITCHEN BLESSING

(Saint Brigid is credited with composing the following prayer to bless her kitchen.)

My kitchen,

The kitchen of the White God,

A kitchen which my King hath blessed,

A kitchen stocked with butter.

Mary's Son, my friend, come thou

To bless my kitchen.

The Prince of the World to the boarder,

May He bring abundance with Him.[4]

—Attributed to Saint Brigid

NOTES

[1] Michael Staunton, *The Voice of the Irish* (Mahwah, N.J.: Hidden Spring), p. 48.

[2] Courtney Davis, *The Book of Celtic Saints* (New York: Blandfords), p. 32.

[3] *Butler's Lives of the Saints, Volume 1* (New York: P.J. Kenedy and Sons, 1963), p. 227.

[4] Nigel Pennick, *The Celtic Saints* (New York: Sterling, 1997), p. 21.

notes

saint isidore the farmer

PATRON SAINT OF:

Peasants,

Farmers

and

Day Laborers

Born: circa 1070

Died: May 15, 1130

FEAST DAY:

May 15

isidore: the simple farmer

The legends surrounding Saint Isidore's life are as rich and plentiful as the golden wheat he farmed in Madrid. However, the facts surrounding his life are much more mundane—some might even say tragic—but nevertheless telling of what a true saint Isidore is.

Isidore began each day by attending Mass. Because of his dedication to receiving the Sacrament, he often arrived late to the fields to begin the arduous work. With the hot sun beating down, he harnessed his oxen to plow and then led them through the deep ruts that formed in the crusty earth. As he got into the rhythm of his day, he spent more time speaking with God.

Nothing more than a simple farmer, Isidore was content with his place in the world. He eventually settled down and married a poor girl from his village, Maria Torribia. They had a happy marriage that included Maria giving birth to a little boy. Isidore adored his young son. The family was living the seemingly perfect life until one day the little boy fell into a well. The couple was filled with dread that their son wouldn't survive the accident. Isidore and Maria prayed to God for their son's safety, and soon afterward the water in the well rose to the level of the ground and safely carried the child back to their arms. After their prayers were answered, they vowed a life of abstinence. But despite their devotion and thanksgiving to God, soon after the incident at the well their beloved child died. Instead of getting angry and raging against God, Maria and Isidore accepted God's will. Isidore continued to attend Mass daily and to tend to the fields and pray just as he did before his son died. Though he lived a largely unremarkable life, many legends survive the saint, who died in 1130.

According to one legend, when King Phillip III of Spain was lying on his deathbed, he asked for Isidore's remains to be brought to him. The king felt that the mere presence of the remains would certainly cure him. As it happened, as soon as the remains were dug up, the King began to feel better. By the time Isidore's relics were in the king's presence, he was fully recovered.

Another legend tells of how one morning Isidore's master, Juan de Vargas, sat overlooking the fields and watched as, one by one, each of the laborers arrived. Every worker was there except Isidore. Juan de Vargas didn't like the idea of one of his laborers shorting him work and resolved to confront Isidore as soon as he arrived. As Juan de Vargas walked toward Isidore, he saw a set of snow white oxen with angels shimmering in the distance, plowing side by side with Isidore. At once Juan de Vargas realized that Isidore was getting help from above. Not only was Isidore plowing his fair share, he was plowing more! Another legend tells of how, while out working, Juan de Vargas came up to Isidore and together they began to walk through the fields. Because it was such a hot summer day, Juan de Vargas was so parched he could barely speak. At that very moment from beneath Isidore's feet a fountain of water shot from the arid soil. Juan de Vargas would thirst no more. Juan and Isidore shared a special connection that most humble workers did not have with their masters. At times Isidore was invited to dine at the manor house to share in the rich and healthy foods the master could afford. Sometimes Isidore would stay so late in the fields praying that the dinner was almost completely over. When he would finally put his oxen away and walk to the manor house, behind him would be a trail of hungry beggars hoping for a morsel of food. Finally arriving to dinner, Isidore saw the food was almost all gone, but was not concerned. Together Isidore and the poor beggars sat down and began to eat. Not only was there enough food for Isidore, but there was also more than enough for all of the hungry beggars.

> The well where Saint Isidore's son survived and the spring that exploded beneath Isidore's feet are still in Madrid, and every day many people visit these sights.

REFLECTION

Although the legends are beautiful, and I love the idea of snow-white oxen and angels plowing the fields, I appreciate the more mundane aspects of Saint Isidore's life.

Every day, all day, Saint Isidore made a choice to put God first. By going to Mass daily, he put God first. When he plowed the fields and communed with God, he put God first. When he helped feed the poor, he put God first.

When I think about the choices I make on a daily basis, I don't think I can say I always put God first. Sometimes in my hectic schedule, God takes a backseat. I don't do it on purpose. If someone ever asked me: "What is most important? God or anything else?" I know what the right answer is: "God is most important." But in the everyday, I sometimes forget.

A couple of years ago at Christmas Mass, the priest posed a question during his homily. He asked if everyone had been busy getting ready for Christmas. I had twenty-five people coming to my house for dinner that night. I felt like the poster child for busy. As I sat in the pew reviewing all of the cooking and cleaning and shopping and wrapping I had done over and above all of my daily responsibilities, I began to feel pretty proud of all I had done to prepare for Christmas. That's when the priest lowered the boom. He rephrased his question to "Have you been busy preparing your souls for Christmas?" I didn't sit quite so high in the pew after that question. I thought about how I yelled at the kids just that morning over something trivial. I was stressed about the party, and I took it out on them. I remembered standing in line at the grocery store with a cart full of food while a woman stood behind me with three items. I thought about letting her go ahead of me in line, but I had so many things to do that day that I just couldn't spare the extra five minutes. I am sure I wasted it that night watching some reality TV show. I thought about the times I cut someone off in traffic so I could get somewhere thirty seconds faster. I reflected on the couple times my children invited me to their school Mass during the holidays and I declined because I had too much to do. I had been given several invitations from God to prepare my soul for Christmas, but instead I went shopping. I did not make the time for God like I could have. Saint Isidore put God first even in the busy times and little moments.

I admire the way Saint Isidore prayed with God throughout the day. He continually worked on his relationship with God. It struck me that I write down the goals I want to achieve over the next few years and spend a lot of time figuring out how I will attain them, yet I do not spend time writing down how I am going to make my relationship with God better. I think I will find more moments throughout the day when I can pray a simple prayer to God.

If you just look at the way Saint Isidore lived his life and throw out all of the legends and miracles, he was still a very special person. He lived a very poor, humble life spent focused on God. So many saints I read about accomplished

Saint Isidore's wife is also a canonized saint. She is sometimes called Maria de la Cabeza. This comes from the tradition of parading her head (in Spanish, *cabeza*) down the streets of Spain to ward off drought. Interestingly enough, one summer we had a terrible drought. I had a cement angel in my garden whose head had been broken for several years. I liked the angel, so I kept propping the head on the body instead of throwing it out. With the drought, I told my kids about Saint Maria de la Cabeza, and we decided to place our angel head face up in our garden and to pray to her to intercede for rain. After three consecutive nights of rain and one particularly loud thunderstorm, my son came up to me and said, "Mom, get that head out of the garden!"

marvelous things in their lifetimes. Saint Hildegard wrote many books. Saints Clare and Francis created a whole new method to perform God's work. Saint Isidore did not do big things in his lifetime, but he did small things right. He gives me hope that anyone can attain sainthood. They only need to follow Jesus' teachings to achieve it.

saint isidore and the tapa

Saint Isidore appeared to King Alphonse VIII in a vision to help him defeat the Moors in 1212. King Alphonse VIII is the grandfather of Saint Ferdinand and the great-grandfather of King Alphonse X, who is the originator of the *tapa* (little meals or snacks). Apparently, in the mid- to late-thirteenth century, King Alphonse X was ill and could only eat a little at a time. He decreed that all drinking establishments should serve a little food on top of their bottle of wine or beer. This ensured two things. First, people of low income would get some food to offset the alcohol. Second, the slice of ham or cheese served on top of the bottle of alcohol helped to keep insects and impurities out of the alcohol. (It seems to me the insects and impurities would be all over the ham or cheese, but that is neither here nor there.) The decree soon turned into tradition and now tapas are served all over Spain and in many places in North America.[1]

SAINT ISIDORE'S MANOR HOUSE MEAL

Inspired Menu

In Madrid the rich households could afford to serve meats at their dinners. They would not have served fish because Madrid is too far away from the coast. This is a meal that Saint Isidore might have enjoyed on one of his invitations to Juan de Vargas's manor house. The rustic apple turnovers are easy to carry and something a farmer could enjoy while on break in the fields.

MANOR HOUSE CHICKEN

Serves: 6

Prep time: 10 minutes

Cook time: 35–40 minutes

You will need:

- 2 chorizo sausages (around 1/2 pound), or substitute mild Italian sausage
- 3 pounds chicken pieces with skin and bones (breasts, thighs, legs and wings)
- 1 teaspoon kosher salt
- freshly ground black pepper to taste
- 2 yellow onions, each cut into 6 to 8 wedges
- 6 sprigs fresh thyme
- 6 fresh sage leaves
- 1 bay leaf
- 1 (14-ounce) can artichoke hearts, drained
- 10 ounces "baby bella" or button mushrooms, cleaned and stems removed, quartered
- 2 tablespoons flour
- 2 cups dry white wine (such as Pinot Grigio)

Remove sausages from their casings and cut into 1/2-inch coins. Place the sausage coins into a large 12-inch skillet with high sides. (If you do not own a large skillet, split the ingredients into two smaller skillets.) Cut the chicken breasts in half so that all the chicken pieces are similar in size. Season the chicken pieces on both sides with salt and pepper. Place the chicken pieces skin side down on top of the sausage coins into a large 12-inch skillet with high sides. Wedge the onions in between the chicken so that a part of the onions are touching the bottom of the pan. Add thyme, sage and bay leaf to the skillet. Cook over medium-high heat for 5–10 minutes until the chicken, sausage and onion mixture begins to caramelize (or brown). Turn the chicken and sausage over for even caramelization and cook for another 5 minutes. Sprinkle the flour over the chicken mixture and lightly toss the chicken mixture. Add artichokes, mushrooms and wine. Cover skillet and lower heat to medium low. Cook for 25 minutes. This recipe can be prepared a day or two ahead and kept refrigerated and then reheated before serving.

Polenta With Romesco Sauce

Romesco Sauce

Serves: 6

Prep time: 10 minutes

Cook time: 15 minutes

You will need:

    1/4 cup toasted almonds

    1 tablespoon olive oil

    2 cloves smashed garlic

    2 (12-ounce) jars roasted red peppers

    1 cup chopped onions

    1 tablespoons red wine vinegar

    2 tablespoons dry white wine

    1/4 teaspoons salt

    freshly ground black pepper to taste

    optional garnish: chopped Spanish green olives stuffed with anchovies

Place the almonds into a food processor. Pulse on and off for 30 seconds and set aside. Put olive oil and garlic into a large skillet over low heat for 10 minutes, stirring occasionally. Remove the garlic from the pan and place into the food processor with the almonds and pulse for about 30 seconds. Add the red pepper and pulse until a somewhat smooth salsa forms (about 1 minute). Make it more or less smooth to your preference. Set this aside. In the skillet with the oil, add the onions and turn heat to high. Stir occasionally until the onions caramelize (turn brown), but don't burn (about 5 minutes). Add the vinegar, wine, red pepper paste, and salt and pepper. Stir until all is combined. Let this sit while you prepare the polenta.

Polenta

Serves: 6

Prep time: 5 minutes

Cook time: 5–10 minutes

You will need:

    1 (14-ounce) can chicken broth

    14 ounces whole milk

    2 torn fresh sage leaves

    1 cup instant polenta

    1/2 cup freshly grated Parmesano-Reggiano cheese

Tip: To save any leftover polenta, place it on a large piece of plastic wrap and cover entirely. Shape the polenta into a cube. Store in the refrigerator. When ready to use again, slice the polenta and fry in a tablespoon of olive oil over medium heat.

In a large saucepan bring broth, milk and sage leaves to a boil. Whisk in polenta until it thickens (this happens quickly). Stir in the cheese. Serve immediately. Pour the Romesco sauce over the polenta. Sprinkle with Spanish olives if desired.

Isidore's Peasant Apple Turnover

Serves: 6

Prep time: 25 minutes

Cook time: 20–25 minutes

Preheat oven: 375° F

Crust

You will need:

>   2 2/3 cups flour
>
>   2 teaspoons sugar
>
>   1 teaspoon salt
>
>   1 cup vegetable shortening
>
>   1/2 cup ice-cold water

In a large bowl blend dry ingredients. Cut in vegetable shortening with a pastry cutter or, alternatively, use two knives and cut criss-cross into the flour shortening mixture until a coarse, pea-sized meal is formed. Use a fork to mix in the water. Form into 6 balls. Place the dough in the refrigerator. When ready to insert filling, roll into 1/2-inch thick circles on a floured surface so the crusts will not stick. You may need to sprinkle a little flour on top of the dough as well so it does not stick to the rolling pin.

Filling

You will need:

>   1 large Granny Smith apple, peeled and cut into 1/2-inch cubes
>
>   1 large Golden Delicious apple, peeled and chopped into pea-sized pieces
>
>   (The combined cut apples should total about three cups.)
>
>   1/4 cup brown sugar
>
>   1/2 teaspoon cinnamon
>
>   1 tablespoon flour

In a large bowl combine the apples, brown sugar, cinnamon and flour until all of the apples are fully coated. Place about 1/2 cup of the apple mixture on the lower half of a dough circle. Gently fold over the other half to enclose it.

Pinch the sides together and then press the edges together with the tines of a fork. Place the turnovers on a large ungreased baking sheet so that they are not touching each other. Poke the turnovers with a fork a couple of times to let steam leave the filling. Bake 20–25 minutes until the turnovers are a golden brown. Place the turnovers on a cookie rack to cool off.

Glaze

You will need:

- 1 tablespoon butter, melted
- 1 teaspoon vanilla extract
- 1 tablespoon milk
- 1 cup powdered sugar

In a medium bowl mix butter, vanilla, milk and powdered sugar. Stir with the back of a spoon, pressing the icing against the sides of the bowl to press out all of the lumps. Drizzle the glaze over the turnover and then spread it to lightly cover the entire tart. Repeat until all of the turnovers are glazed.

DINNER CONVERSATION

Copy the following questions on pieces of paper and put them in a bowl and place on the table. While people are eating, pass the bowl around and have each person pull out a question. Everyone can take a turn answering the questions.

1. Can you think of times in your life when God has taken a back seat?
2. Can you think of times during your day when you could pray with God?
3. Have you had any experiences in your life that you could describe as a miracle?
4. What are some ways that you can work on your relationship with God?
5. How do you keep God first in your life?

SAINT ISIDORE'S MEAL PRAYER

Spirit of the Living God, throughout these coming days I ask you to open my heart to discover your presence. Plant seeds of stillness and discernment within me. Help my vision and awareness grow to discover how you are already present and awaiting me in my daily life and dreams. Water me with gentleness and compassion. Prune away any unnecessary action and hardness of my heart. Allow me to blossom with reverence for all of creation and allow me to mature in depth of forgiveness, mercy and deeds for others. I trust you and bless you, granting you permission to transform me into your heart's desire.

Master Gardener, you created the world and desire that I love you with all my mind, heart and soul. Show me how.

Master Gardener, you are already present in every moment of my daily life. Teach me to discover and appreciate your presence in the people and places I encounter every day.

Master Gardener, you will come alive more fully in my life when I surrender to your loving will and design for my life that we create together. Allow me to give you permission to transform me into your ambassador on earth.[2]

—*Pegge Bernecker*, Your Spiritual Garden

NOTES

[1] The Web site www.arrakis.es by Yolanda Maria Vicente has a wonderful history of how tapas are made and how they came to be named.

[2] Pegge Bernecker, *Your Spiritual Garden: Tending to the Presence of God: A Six-Week Daily Life Retreat* (Cincinnati: St. Anthony Messenger, 2006), pp. 17–18.

notes

saint margaret
of scotland

PATRON SAINT OF:

Large Families,

Those Mourning the Death of a Child,

Education and Learning,

Scotland,

Widows

and

Queens

Born: circa 1045

Died: November 16, 1093

FEAST DAY:

November 16 (formerly celebrated on June 10)

margaret: queen of charity

In 1016 the Danish took control of England. The English royal family was in grave danger and had no choice but to take their young children across the turbulent sea to Hungary for refuge. There they were welcomed to live in the royal court of King Peter Urseolo. This Hungarian castle offered all of the finer things. There were beautiful tapestries hung on the walls that not only made the castle more beautiful, but warmer too. Sparkling silver trays served aromatic meals. The ladies of the court wore colorful gowns and were covered in jewels. Aristocratic young ladies were trained in Latin, German and English and were taught all of the Christian virtues.

Saint Margaret was born into this royal English family that exiled in Hungary. She, too, learned all of the finer things the court had to teach, and she grew to be an intelligent, refined, devout, young lady. She appreciated the generosity of the Hungarian court and fully knew her life depended upon their kindness. By the time she was twelve, the political climate in England had changed. Her great-uncle was the king and her family once again ruled England. Margaret and her family traveled the long journey back to England to live in the English court and wait for the day that her own father would become king.

The family quickly adjusted to their new life and enjoyed feeling in control of their destiny. Shortly after they settled, Margaret's father fell ill and died. And in 1066 William the Conqueror invaded England and won the throne in the infamous Battle of Hastings. Again Margaret's family was no longer safe. So under the cover of darkness, the family headed for their ship and made haste for Hungary. The seas were torturous and the frigid winds were fierce. The ship blew up the coast to Dunfermline, Scotland, where it landed at what is now called St. Margaret's Hope.

Malcolm III, the king of Scotland, greeted the family and took them in. Scotland and England had been battling for years, and Malcolm could see the benefit of an alliance with England. Malcolm, a powerful and cunning leader, immediately felt an attraction to Margaret. He respected her intelligence and admired her inner beauty as well as her delicate frame. But he was the opposite of her. He was large, uneducated and almost savage. He wanted her as his bride, and with the situation her family was in, she acquiesced. Margaret soon found Malcolm's inner goodness and returned his love. At twenty-four, she knew this foreign land was now her country. She wanted to make her surroundings more familiar, so she began to bring some of the finer things into her new court. She hung beautiful tapestries, dressed in the latest couture and introduced ornate silver serving items. The castle was now a place where a king could entertain influential people.

As Margaret looked around the kingdom, she felt so much unrest and strife. She longed for her people to get along and treat each other with the respect Jesus taught. To incite change, she began with herself. During Lent and Advent she began each day before dawn praying and attending several Masses. She fasted through the day and then before she would eat her one paltry meal, she would personally feed poor orphans who had been brought to the castle. She would pray some more, then before retiring to bed, she and the king would wash the feet of some chosen poor people in the kingdom. They then would provide them with food and money to help their families. Together Margaret and Malcolm would host large feasts for the three hundred most destitute villagers in the kingdom. The great hall was filled with tables set with the finest silver. The food was delicious and bountiful. Anyone walking in would think the feast was for the richest nobility in the kingdom, not the poorest peasants. No one else was allowed to attend or witness this act of generosity. This was not a public relations stunt to impress; it was their gift. The couple served the food lovingly to the poor as though they were serving Jesus himself.

As Margaret grew spiritually, she began to affect others around her. It was the most evident in her husband. Before Margaret's arrival into his life, he had never held feasts for the poor, and wouldn't even think of washing someone else's feet. As he witnessed her inner peace grow, he began to join in her charity. Others began to help, too. Margaret picked the best embroiderers in the court and joined them in the task of creating golden-flecked altar cloths for the church she had built in Dunfermline.

Some people, however, were more difficult to convince and needed a little prodding before they changed their ways. Margaret made it a custom to say grace before and after dinner, but some of the knights left the table immediately after finishing dinner—without so much as a thank-you. Margaret didn't like the fact that they didn't thank the Lord after their meal, so she instituted the grace cup. A bejeweled silver cup with handles on either side was filled with fine wine and placed on the table at the end of the meal. Anyone who stayed and said the final grace could partake of the wine. The knights, not wanting to pass up another glass of wine, soon began praying after each meal.

This is a tradition that continues today in Scotland.

Slowly but surely, Margaret's influence began to spread. The people in her court were praying more and becoming more generous. Now she wanted to give all of Scotland more access to salvation. It was common for everyday people to go on pilgrimages to shrines and religious places. It was the belief that at such a holy place only good things could happen. All ills would be healed. All prayers would be answered. Saint Margaret provided easier access to Saint Andrew's shrine in Scotland. She had hostels built and staffed so pilgrims would have a comfortable place to stay and good food to eat. She provided a boat to ferry people across the river to the shrine. The ferry that runs there today is called the Queensferry to honor Saint Margaret. She hosted synods where she encouraged changes that brought the Scottish church in line with the Roman church. During the Middle Ages most people felt they were not worthy of receiving Holy Communion. Margaret wanted the people to experience the joy of the Eucharist, so she suggested confession and penance as the path to cleanse the soul and make ready for the Eucharist. This was a radical shift in thought for the times. People slowly began to share her view.

In 1093 Malcolm and two of their sons went to battle against England. Margaret was sick and begged them not to go. Duty called, and they went against her wishes. As she lay in bed, feeling particularly morose, her son Edgar came back from the battlefield. Some time passed before he could find the words to tell his mother that Malcolm and Edward, his older brother, were killed. After all of her struggles in life, this was more than she could handle. After hearing the news, Margaret began to pray, "Lord Jesus, Who according to the will of the Father, through the co-operation of the Holy Ghost, hast by Thy death given life to the world, deliver me...."[1] With that, Saint Margaret died.

all in the family

Saint Margaret had many saintly connections. On her mother's side she was related to Saints Henry and Cunegund. Saint Stephen had been the king of Hungary and was responsible for the Christian disposition of the court. He died shortly before he appointed Peter Urseolo to the throne and Saint Margaret arrived in Hungary. Saint Margaret's son David is also a canonized saint.

REFLECTION

It is amazing the impact Saint Margaret had on her country. She made great changes, but she started small. So many times I think I cannot effect great change because I am not in a position that will affect a lot of people. At first glance it seems obvious that as queen, Saint Margaret could impact many lives. She didn't mandate change, but inspired it with small actions that rippled like a drop of rain falling into a puddle. If I take Saint Margaret's lead and start with myself, maybe my children will follow my example. Maybe my actions can have a similar ripple effect.

Today we talk a lot about character. Someone once defined character as "doing the right thing when no one is looking." Saint Margaret embodied that definition. She recognized people in need and helped them because it was the right thing to do. She didn't always parade her good acts in front of everyone. Sometimes she performed her acts of charity publicly to incite change, but other times she acted quietly, just for God to witness.

> [Jesus] also said, "With what can we compare the kingdom of God, or what parable will we use for it? It is like a mustard seed, which, when sown upon the ground, is the smallest of all seeds on earth; yet when it is sown it grows up and becomes the greatest of all shrubs, and puts forth large branches, so that the birds of the air can make nests in its shade." (Mark 4:30–32)

SAINT MARGARET'S CHARITY SOUP MEAL

Inspired Menu

I first tasted a version of this soup when a dear friend of mine, Christy Pucci, out of charity, made it for my family after I gave birth to my youngest child, Charley. My family loved it, and while I loved the soup, too, I have to admit I mostly loved having a break during such a hectic time. Now when I make this for my family (with my own additions to Christy's original recipe), I always make a batch for someone else who might need a pick-me-up. And I can't help but think of Saint Margaret and her own charity. This hearty soup honors the times when Saint Margaret turned her home into a soup kitchen to feed the needy.

Every time I use mustard seeds in recipes (which I do in the salad dressing in this meal) I am reminded of the parable of the mustard seed and how our deeds, small like a mustard seed, can grow into the most marvelous actions with faith, hope, charity and love. The dessert is rich, decadent and worthy of a king—or three hundred of the neediest people in his kingdom!

Saint Margaret's Charity Meatball Tortellini Soup

Serves: 10–12

Prep time: 40 minutes

Cook time: 45 minutes

Preheat oven: 350° F

Time saver: Instead of making homemade meatballs for the soup, buy frozen meatballs. They will be a little larger, but still good.

Meatballs

You will need:

- 1/2 pound ground sirloin
- 1/2 pound ground pork
- 1/2 cup Italian bread crumbs
- 3/4 cup Parmesan cheese
- 1 egg
- 1/2 teaspoon ground pepper

Put all of the ingredients into a large bowl and gently mix with your hands. Once combined, roll into balls about the size of an acorn. Place on a baking sheet that has sides and bake for 15 minutes. Set aside.

Soup

You will need:

- 1 batch of cooked meatballs (see previous recipe)
- 1 medium-sized yellow onion, chopped
- 1 stalk of celery, chopped (about 1/3 cup)
- 1 tablespoon olive oil
- 3 (32-ounce) cans chicken broth
- 1 1/2 cups carrots sliced into 1/2-inch coins
- 1 bay leaf
- 1 (14.5-ounce) can petite-cut tomatoes
- 1/4 teaspoon dried basil
- 1/2 teaspoon minced garlic
- 1 1/2 cups frozen baby peas
- 1 bag frozen cheese tortellini

In a large soup pot, sauté onions and celery in olive oil over medium heat for 5–10 minutes. The onions should be translucent. Add chicken broth, carrots, bay leaf, tomatoes, and meatballs and garlic. Bring to a boil and cook on medium for 10 minutes. When the carrots are al dente, add basil, peas and tortellini. Bring to a boil again and cook for another 7 minutes until the tortellini is cooked.

SAINT CHRISTINE'S OVEN-BAKED BREAD

Serves: 6

Prep time: 30 minutes

Cook time: 25 minutes

Preheat oven: 350° F

You will need:

> 1 pound frozen bread dough, thawed to room temperature (It may take a couple of hours to thaw completely enough to roll out.)
>
> 1 (4-ounce) tub garlic herb cheese spread, such as allouette or boursin cheese
>
> 1 egg white
>
> 1 tablespoon sesame seed (optional)

Place the dough on a greased baking sheet. Roll the dough into a large rectangle (about 8 x 14 inches). Spread the cheese over the dough. Taking the long edge of the dough, roll over onto itself. Keep rolling until you meet the other side of the dough. When finished, the dough should form a long cylinder. Brush the outside of the dough with egg whites, then sprinkle with sesame seeds. Cover with plastic wrap and let rise for about 25 minutes. Bake for 25 minutes until the bread is a golden brown.

going crazy in the kitchen? christine can help!

Saint Christine was a twelfth-century saint who suffered a grand mal seizure, and everyone thought she was dead. At her funeral Mass, she awoke and flew to the ceiling to escape the scent of human sin from the people in the church. Her sister and the priest talked her down from the ceiling, but Christine spent the rest of her life hiding in ovens and other places to escape from overpowering odors. She is now the patron saint of psychiatrists and those with mental illnesses and—more loosely interpreted—anyone going nuts in the kitchen.

SCOTLAND SPRING SALAD WITH MUSTARD SEED DRESSING

Serves: 6

Prep time: 10 minutes

Cook time: 5–10 minutes

Salad

You will need:

    1 (5-ounce) bag of spring greens

    6 large strawberries, cleaned and sliced

    1 ripe avocado, sliced

    1/4 cup toasted macadamia nuts

    1/4 cup goat cheese or blue cheese crumbles

When ready to serve the salad, place the greens, strawberries, avocado, cheese and nuts in a salad bowl and drizzle dressing over the salad. Toss to mix. (The avocados and strawberries will be fresher if sliced right before serving.)

Dressing

You will need:

3/4 cup sweet onion, chopped

3 tablespoons olive oil, divided

1 tablespoon whole grain mustard (mustard made with whole mustard seed)

2 tablespoons honey

1 tablespoon lemon juice

salt and pepper to taste

Place onions and 1 tablespoon olive oil into a medium saucepan over medium-high heat. Stir occasionally so the onions brown, but not burn. Cook for 5–10 minutes until the onions are soft and caramelized.

Place the onions and oil from the pan into a jar or container that has a lid. Add the remaining oil, mustard, honey, lemon juice, salt and pepper. Place the lid on the jar and shake well to combine.

FIT FOR A KING CHOCOLATE MINT CREAM CAKES

Yields: 24 mini cakes

Prep time: 30 minutes

Cook time: 15 minutes

Preheat oven: 350° F

Cakes

You will need:

1/2 cup buttermilk

1/2 cup water

1/3 cup canola oil

1 teaspoon peppermint extract

1 cup sugar

1 egg

1/2 teaspoon baking soda

1 cup all-purpose flour

1/3 cup unsweetened cocoa powder

In a large bowl combine buttermilk, water, oil, peppermint extract, sugar, egg and baking soda. Mix on low speed with mixer for 2 minutes. Add flour and cocoa powder and mix for another 2 minutes. Divide batter into 24 greased muffin rounds. Bake for 15 minutes. The cakes are ready when you lightly press your finger on them and they slowly spring back. Let the cakes sit in the pan for 5 minutes before removing to cool completely on a wire rack.

Vanilla Cream Filling
You will need:

    4 ounces cream cheese, softened

    1 (3.4-ounce) package of instant vanilla pudding mix

    1 cup whipping cream

In a large bowl mix cream cheese, pudding mix and whipping cream for 2–3 minutes.

Scoop this mixture into a large plastic zip-top storage bag. Squeeze the cream mixture toward one corner of the bag. Cut that corner of the bag to make a ½-inch opening. Set aside.

Chocolate Ganache
You will need:

    1 cup whipping cream

    8 ounces high-quality semisweet chocolate chips

Bring cream to a slow boil over medium-high heat, stirring constantly. Remove from heat and whisk in chocolate chips until the cream and chocolate form a smooth sauce.

To assemble the cakes, slice a cupcake in half horizontally. In a circular motion, starting on the outer edge of the bottom half of the cupcake, squeeze the vanilla cream mixture to cover the bottom half of the cake. Place the top half of the cake over the vanilla cream. Place the cake on wax paper and pour about 1 tablespoon of ganache over the cake. It is easiest to put this together in an assembly line fashion. Cut all of the cakes open first. Swirl the cream filling on the bottom halves next. Finally, place the tops over the cream and cover with chocolate ganache.

Optional Garnish

    Reddi-Wip whipped topping

    24 mint sprigs

If desired, place a dollop of Reddi-Wip on top of each cake and top with a fresh mint sprig.

DINNER CONVERSATION

Copy the following questions on pieces of paper and put them in a bowl and place on the table. While people are eating, pass the bowl around and have each person pull out a question. Everyone can take a turn answering the questions.

1. Can you think of times in your own life when things didn't go as you had hoped or planned, but in time you grew to appreciate or accept the fate you were given?
2. Can you think of a small act that you or someone you know did to affect a big change?
3. So many people of great wealth and stature use their position to gain more wealth and stature for themselves. Margaret's story is so beautiful and memorable, because it is so rare. Or is it? Can you think of people in today's world with both wealth and stature who have reached out to help the less fortunate?
4. Saint Margaret was able to gently nudge people into doing the right thing. Can you think of examples when you or someone you know have done the same?

SAINT MARGARET'S MEAL PRAYER

Dear Saint Margaret, your actions of love, compassion and charity were indeed like the tiny mustard seed. They were the seemingly small and insignificant actions of one person, yet these acts of kindness grew in the hearts of many. May all our actions, small and not so small, be carried forward and spread throughout all of humankind.

NOTE
[1] Elizabeth Whitehead, *Saints for the Married* (Liverpool: Mercier, 1949), p. 90.

notes

saint hildegard
of bingen

Patron Saint of:

Abbesses,

Herbalists,

Gardeners,

Healers,

Writers

and

Composers

Born: circa 1098

Died: September 17, 1179

Feast day:

September 17

hildegard: ahead of her time

During the Middle Ages people followed many customs that we find incomprehensible today. We wouldn't think of bloodletting as a means to cure an illness and, regardless of famine, we would never sell human flesh in the market. But in the Middle Ages lots of these unfathomable practices existed. In fact, it was also fairly common for wealthy noble families to give their young children (along with a sizable donation) to an abbey to be raised. Saint Hildegard was no exception, and at the age of eight her parents sent her to live at the abbey with monks and nuns in Disibodenberg, Germany. How frightened she must have been to leave her family and live in a strange place with people she barely knew!

Hildegard managed to find her way and soon realized she was called to the religious life. At age fourteen, when most girls her age were getting married, Hildegard took her religious vows and became a nun. For the next several years Hildegard lived much the same as the other nuns. It wasn't until she was forty-two that she experienced a deeper conversion to Christ. She writes:

> Heaven was opened and a fiery light of exceeding brilliance came and permeated my whole brain, and inflamed my whole heart and breast...like a warming flame, as the sun warms anything its rays touch. And immediately I knew the meaning of the exposition of the scriptures, namely the Psalter, the Gospel, and the other Catholic volumes of both the Old and New Testaments.[1]

Since childhood, Hildegard had experienced visions, but she kept them to herself. She knew that even the most religious people would question the sanity of a person who believed she was receiving such explicit messages straight from God. Hildegard might have kept this vision quiet too, but she received a directive from God to share this message. She didn't immediately start writing God's word. There wasn't much precedent for a twelfth-century woman to write at all, let alone with authority on God. Discreetly, she wrote down her visions and shared them with a monk at the abbey, who reviewed them and determined they were from God. He shared her visions with his abbot who in turn shared them with his higher-ups. Eventually, Pope Eugenius III became an audience to her writings and declared publicly that she should write down everything she saw or heard in a vision.

So at age forty-three, Saint Hildegard began the laborious task of writing down her visions, which took ten years to complete. Under her instruction, a monk transcribed her writings onto parchment and illuminated her visions into pictures. Because bookmaking was so time-consuming and costly, only the most important writings were made into books. It is amazing to think that a woman in the twelfth century was given this approval.

News of Hildegard's visions spread quickly, and with Hildegard's newfound fame people from across the land requested her assistance. Bishops, popes and heads of nations sent letters to Hildegard asking her opinion on many matters. She was very comfortable speaking her opinion to these powerful men. If she felt they were not being Christian, she didn't hesitate to reprimand them.

Following in Hildegard's footsteps, many young women decided to take their vows and join the abbey, and along with them came large donations from their wealthy families. Soon Hildegard attained the position of abbess and realized the nuns needed more room than they were allotted at Disibodenberg. When she asked for permission to separate the convent from the friary, the brothers tried to stop the move. They didn't want to lose the fame and money Hildegard's status brought to them. The brothers eventually relented, and Hildegard and her sisters started building their new abbey in Rupertsberg.

It was here in Rupertsberg that Hildegard tended her herb garden. She knew the smell, taste and look of each plant. She spent time drying, boiling and steeping various herbs together to find the perfect curative powers to heal the sisters' ailments. She knew the importance of proper medicine to heal the body, but deeply believed in the power of prayer as well. The Scriptures are full of examples of Jesus healing medical ailments as well as saving people's souls. Hildegard understood that both things are necessary.

With the sun soaking into her skin, Hildegard sat on the grounds of her beautiful new abbey and wrote joyous songs in praise of the saints and God. Without any formal training, she wrote mini-operas in the new style of music with singing and musical instruments joined together. Hildegard explains, "[T]he words symbolize the body, and the jubilant music indicates the spirit; and the celestial harmony shows the Divinity, and the words the Humanity of the Son of God."[2] High on a hill in colorful dresses and crowned in jewels, the sisters of the abbey joyfully harmonized the praises Hildegard had written. Softly the voices floated down to the valley and river below for all to enjoy.

Hildegard spent her later years writing and traveling through Europe preaching. Throughout this time, however, she grew increasingly ill and suffered from pain. She described her ordeal as if she was *"being baked as it were in an oven....* However racked I was by these things, still, I continued dictating, singing, and writing through the heavenly vision whatever the Holy Spirit wished to announce through me."[3] Just as Hildegard appreciated all of the beautiful things God created for us, she accepted the pain as a gift from God. She saw goodness in it and used prayer and the Scriptures to help her through it.

At the end of her life Hildegard experienced one final trial. An excommunicated nobleman had been buried on the grounds of the abbey. Hildegard's superiors told her he must be removed from the hallowed grounds immediately. She declined, stating that the man had confessed his sins and received absolution and last rites. Not liking her act of defiance, her superiors retaliated by placing an interdict on the abbey, which barred Hildegard and the other nuns from participating in the sacraments. For a community that loved to celebrate God through music and Eucharist, this was a terrible blow. The sisters followed the restraints of the interdict, and left the nobleman buried on the abbey grounds. Hildegard pleaded her case until finally the archbishop of Mainz concurred with Hildegard and removed the interdict. Six months later on September 17, 1179, Saint Hildegard died.

Although elected for canonization four times, Hildegard has never been formally canonized in the Catholic church. While not an official saint, she is nevertheless renowned or called saint and venerated as one throughout the world, especially in Germany. She is not the official patron saint of any one thing, however, her work as an abbess, herbalist, gardener, healer, writer and composer inspires many and lights the way for followers throughout the world.

REFLECTION

Saint Hildegard's writings about herbs and plants initially attracted me to her. After learning more, I discovered so many other admirable aspects of her personality. Through music and art she celebrated the good, and with the help of the Scriptures she embraced the suffering. As my mother was dying, she chose to embrace death, too. She listened joyfully to the music the hospice caregiver played, and she offered up her pain to those in need. Watching my mother and father accept death as a part of life helped make it easier for me to watch my mother die, and it also strengthened me for the time when she would not be here with me.

I like picturing Hildegard in quiet meditation and prayer, and listening to God's voice. In my house I am often so busy with the tasks of the day that I don't take time to sit and give my full focus to God. I pray daily, but many times it is with so many distractions in the background that my prayer is more like a letter to God than a conversation. Jeanne Hunt, author of *Holy Bells and Wonderful Smells*, suggests proclaiming a desert day, fasting from all noise and telephone, and instead she suggests, "Spend some extra time listening to God's voice in this quiet day."[4] For me a whole day of peace is difficult to achieve. (I am less like Hildegard and more like Saint Martha.) A five- to ten-minute daily respite is more attainable for me, yet still very powerful.

Hildegard, for all her time spent singing and meditating, was remarkably prolific. Once she chose to follow God's directive, nothing stopped her. Without a formal education she wrote several books, seventy-seven songs and over three hundred letters, many directed to popes and leaders of countries.

Like Hildegard, we have all been given wonderful gifts from God, but how often do we use our gifts? If ever my confidence is low, I think of Saint Hildegard and realize that with God, I can accomplish anything.

For me, Saint Hildegard is a wonderful inspiration. I think of her often—in simple tasks like creating a healthy meal or deciding to take ten minutes out of my day for focused prayer. When I hear a beautiful song on the radio that fills my soul I can celebrate the gifts God gives us. Saint Hildegard was not only a woman ahead of her time, but a woman for all time.

SAINT HILDEGARD'S HEALING THE SOUL FOOD

Inspired Menu

This inspired meal celebrates Saint Hildegard's message of feeding the body healthy food to maintain a proper balance. In many of the recipes below, I have incorporated many of the ingredients that Hildegard wrote about in her book *Physica*.

HILDEGARD'S FILLET OF "SOUL" WITH GARLIC AND HERBS

Serves: 6

Prep time: 5 minutes

Cook time: 11 minutes

Preheat oven: 450° F

You will need:

> 3 pounds fresh sole fillets
>
> 2 cloves minced garlic
>
> 1/2 teaspoon kosher salt
>
> freshly cracked black pepper to taste
>
> 1/2 cup chopped fresh flat-leaf parsley
>
> 2 lemons, sliced into 1/3-inch thick disks
>
> 1 cup dry white wine (such as Pinot Grigio)

Place the filets in a 9 x 13-inch baking dish in a single layer. Evenly distribute minced garlic on top of fillets. Sprinkle salt and pepper over fillets. Shower the fillets with chopped parsley. Place 2 lemon rounds on top of each fillet. Pour wine around the sides of the fillets. Bake for 9–11 minutes until the fish flakes easily and is opaque.

POTATOES AND LEEKS

Serves: 6

Prep time: 10 minutes

Cook time: 12 minutes

Preheat oven: 450° F

You will need:

> 5 red potatoes
>
> 3 leeks
>
> 2 tablespoons olive oil, divided
>
> 1/2 teaspoon kosher salt, divided
>
> 1/2 teaspoon freshly cracked black pepper, divided
>
> 1/2 cup shredded Parmesan cheese

Spray 2 baking sheets with no-stick cooking spray. Slice the potatoes very thinly (about 1/16 inch). A mandolin slicer or food processor works very well for this task. Spread the potatoes across the 2 baking trays. Drizzle the potatoes with one tablespoon of olive oil and sprinkle with salt and pepper. Bake for 5 to 10 minutes until the potatoes become a light golden brown on top. Use a spatula to turn the potatoes over then layer the leeks over top of the potatoes and sprinkle with some more salt and pepper. Drizzle the potatoes and leeks with the remaining olive oil then sprinkle with shredded Parmesan. Bake for 6 minutes.

SAINT HILDEGARD SALAD

Serves: 6

Prep time: 15 minutes

Dressing

> 2 tablespoons orange juice
>
> 3 tablespoons olive oil
>
> 1 tablespoon honey
>
> 1 clove garlic, minced
>
> 1 tablespoon Dijon mustard
>
> 1 teaspoon red wine vinegar
>
> dash of salt and freshly cracked black pepper

Combine all ingredients in a jar with a lid and shake well. Add to mixed salad just before ready to serve.

Salad

You will need:

> 1 small Granny Smith apple
>
> 1/2 cup orange juice
>
> 2 bulbs fresh fennel
>
> 1 (5-ounce) bag mixed spring salad greens
>
> 2 ounces goat cheese
>
> 1/4 cup toasted sliced almonds
>
> 1/2 cup sliced red onions

Slice Granny Smith apple into very thin disks (about 1/16-inch thick), combine with fennel and pour orange juice over and set in refrigerator while preparing the rest of the salad. Just before ready to serve take apples and fennel out of orange juice and combine with mixed greens, cheese, almonds, onions and dressing.

Saint Hildegard believed that cinnamon and almond bring joy.[8]

JOYFUL COOKIES
Yields: 4 dozen cookies
Prep time: 15 minutes
Cook time: 20 minutes
Preheat oven: 350° F

You will need:
  1/2 cup (1 stick) unsalted butter
  1/2 cup (1 stick) margarine
  1 1/4 cup granulated sugar
  2 egg whites
  1 1/2 teaspoons vanilla extract
  1/2 teaspoon almond extract
  2 1/2 cups all-purpose flour
  1 teaspoon baking soda
  1 teaspoon salt
  1 teaspoon cinnamon
  1/2 cup blanched, slivered almonds

In a large bowl cream butter and sugar until smooth. Add egg whites, vanilla and almond extract and mix until fully combined. Sift flour, baking soda, salt and cinnamon together and then add to butter mixture. Mix on low until everything is fully combined. Stir in almonds until they are fully incorporated into the batter. Spoon heaping tablespoons of dough onto an ungreased cookie sheet. Place the spoonfuls about 2 inches apart. Bake for 10–12 minutes until the cookies are a golden brown.

Saint Blaise's feast day is celebrated on February 3. He is invoked for many reasons, one of which is for a healthy throat. Most likely this stems from a legend that says a young boy was choking on a fish bone and Saint Blaise saved him. Each year on his feast day thousands of people flock to Catholic churches to have their throats blessed.

Saint Blaise Tea

Yields: 1 tea bag

Prep time: 5 minutes

Cook time: 6 minutes

You will need:

  1 (4 x 4 inch square) cheese cloth

  1 teaspoon peppermint flakes

  1/4 teaspoon dried chamomile

  1/4 teaspoon dried lavender

  1/4 teaspoon dried lemon peel

  1 piece of crystallized ginger

  1 (6-inch) piece cooking twine

  10 ounces boiling water

  1 tablespoon honey

Place the cheesecloth on a flat surface. In the center of the cheesecloth place the remaining ingredients with the exception of the twine. Carefully draw up the side if the cheesecloth around the herbs to form a closed ball. Tie this with the twine. Place the tea bag in a mug and pour in boiling water. Let the tea steep for 6 minutes and add the honey. The warm tea with lemon and honey should soothe a dry throat.

Dinner Conversation

Copy the following questions on pieces of paper and put them in a bowl and place on the table. While people are eating, pass the bowl around and have each person pull out a question. Everyone can take a turn answering the questions.

1. Can you think of a painful time in your life that made you grow?

2. What are some of the gifts God has bestowed on you?

3. Are you using your gifts from God? If not, what is stopping you?

4. Name some everyday places where you find God.

5. Can you think of times when you felt you were doing what God wants of you, but you were finding much opposition along the way? How did it turn out in the end?

SAINT HILDEGARD'S MEAL PRAYER
The Image of God

His hair is like the sunset,
His eyes the stars above,
His head's always above the clouds,
His face is full of love.

His body is the Universe,
And all the space between,
His legs are different galaxies,
The most gorgeous ones you've seen.

His toes are different planets,
Just orbiting around,
His fingers are the asteroids,
Which I see that you have found.
His tears are falling comets,

His anger is the sun,
His laughter is the thunder,
When He's having lots of fun!

He is always with us,
In everything we do,
He tells us what is wrong and right,
And helps all of us too.

He's always forgiven us,
For the sins that we have made,
He cleanses all our hearts and souls,
So all the black spots fade.

He has always loved us,
And we have loved Him too,
He is the one and only God,
And He believes in you!

—Abby Heyd, age 10

NOTES
[1] Mother Columbia Hart and Jane Bishop, *Hildegard of Bingen Scivias* (New York: Paulist, 1990), p. 59.
[2] Mother Columbia Hart and Jane Bishop, p. 533.
[3] Anna Silvas, *Jutta & Hildegard: The Biographical Sources* (University Park, Penn.: The Pennsylvania State University Press, 1999), p. 171.
[4] Jeanne Hunt, *Holy Bells and Wonderful Smells* (Cincinnati: St. Anthony Messenger, 1996), p. 32.
[5] Bruce W. Hozeski, *Hildegard's Healing Plants* (Boston: Beacon, 2001), pp. 83–84.
[6] Hozeski, p. 158.
[7] Hozeski, p. 29.
[8] Jany Fournier-Rosset, *From Saint Hildegard's Kitchen, Foods of Health, Foods of Joy* (Ligouri, Mo.: Ligouri, 1999), pp. 27–44.

notes

saint clare of assisi

PATRON SAINT OF:

Embroiderers,

Television,

Difficult Marriages,

Those with Eye Diseases,

Gilders,

Goldsmiths,

Gold Workers,

Good Weather,

Laundry Workers,

Needle Workers,

Telegraphs,

Telephones

Born: July 16, 1194
Died: August 11, 1253

FEAST DAY:

August 11

clare of assisi: persistent, not stubborn

Saint Clare gave up everything to follow in the footsteps of Saint Francis and ultimately Jesus. Born into privilege, her childhood home was a fortress in the center of Assisi. She spent most of her days in rooms specifically designed for women. There she learned to read and write in Italian and French. Dressed in silk and velvet, she and the ladies spent hours embroidering beautiful tapestries. Her home was always pulsing with activity. Her father and uncles were affluent knights. While the ladies were off learning the art of medieval femininity, the men were practicing the art of war. Squires and pages ran about gathering necessities for the great knights, stable boys tended to the horses and cooks prepared glorious feasts. The members of the household gathered together for the feast and then parted ways again. Most likely the men slipped away into the great hall to discuss politics of the time and to determine which male suitors would provide the most beneficial alliance for the family. Clare's uncle was the oldest, so he made most of the final decisions. The fortress ran like a mini-kingdom with Clare's uncle as king.

Outside this fortress the world was slowly changing. For centuries everyone had lived under a feudal system that consisted of two distinct classes. A third, the middle class, began to emerge. The growing trade routes brought new spices, dyes and precious stones to the area. This influx of new imports created new jobs. Some peasants spent their time dying wool and constructing artful fabrics. Others learned the art of blowing glass into elaborate creations. As the peasants perfected their skills, they began selling their wares to the nobles who could afford the extravagant extras. These beautiful luxury items were wonderful signs of the nobility's status, and at the same time the items were the means for peasants to escape poverty and servitude. For the first time peasants could begin to imagine a life other than the filth and sheer poverty their ancestors had to endure for centuries. Clare's household certainly enjoyed the fruits of these tradesmen's labors. They owned spectacular swords with bejeweled handles covered with intricate carvings. The ladies modeled the finest apparel as they attended Mass. Cups, plates and silverware were all specially made for the castles. Even the warhorses enjoyed dressings designed by the tradesmen.

The more freedoms the tradesmen earned the more disparity they recognized between themselves and the nobles. As the peasants began to take control of their lives, they began to fight for more freedoms. Now instead of fighting on behalf of the peasants, the knights were fighting against the peasants. While all this fighting was taking place, Clare's family was forced into exile in Perugia. There she lived with other young noble-born women and forged friendships that lasted her lifetime.

Soon the political climate in Assisi improved enough for the family to move back to their city home. Clare was getting older and the negotiations for her betrothal heightened. One by one available men approached Clare's father and uncle for Clare's hand in marriage. While the men were preoccupied with negotiations, Clare sneaked out of the house to go listen to the traveling friar, Francis of Assisi. When he spoke, it was as if he was speaking directly to her. His ideas were so much like her own. Soon after, they met on several occasions to discuss the Gospels and their beliefs. The two were of one mind.

In the dark of night on Palm Sunday 1212, just before Clare would be forced to accept a marriage proposal, the eighteen-year-old sneaked past the guards at her house and met Saint Francis and some other friars at the church of Santa Maria degli Angeli. She had given her fine gowns and entire dowry to the needy. Dressed in sackcloth and the gray robes of the friars, Clare and Francis stepped onto the altar. Under candlelight, the brothers encircled them and prayed as Francis cut Clare's long silken hair to symbolize her entry into religious life. Immediately, she was taken to the safety of the Convent of St. Paul. Once her family realized her deception, the armed guards charged into the church to reclaim her. She grasped the altar cloths and clung tightly so the guards could not remove her. Finally, she lifted her veil and uncovered her shorn hair. At that, the family realized she would never marry. They acquiesced and three weeks later Clare's younger sister followed a similar path.

Francis' vision was to walk in the way of the Lord. In Luke's Gospel Jesus sent the apostles to proclaim the kingdom of God and to heal, commanding, "Take nothing for your journey, no staff, nor bag, nor bread, nor money—not even an extra tunic. Whatever house you enter, stay there and leave from there" (Luke 9:3). This passage summarizes the Franciscan philosophy. It was very important to Francis to fully live these ideals. As he and his friars went forth preaching, he urged Clare to officially live under the rule of Saint Benedict but in practice to live the ideals she and Francis discussed.

Clare and her followers lived a life of total poverty in their convent at the Church of San Damiano. Shoes and beds were not on the list of necessities. They only ate food found in their backyard garden or given to them as a donation. They spent their days in quiet prayer and humble service. The nuns did not complain about the hardships; they welcomed them. Pope Gregory IX, however, was concerned with the idea of absolute poverty. He seemed to think the idea was a bit naïve and was afraid someone might take advantage of the nuns. When the pope was a cardinal, he set up a rule that allowed the nuns to live in poverty while still maintaining some property. While this was close to the ideals Clare and Francis professed, it still missed the mark. Time and again, Clare approached the pope and asked for the privilege of poverty but was denied.

In 1226 Francis died. Many of his followers continued to adhere to his strict gospel lifestyle; some, however, began to loosen the guidelines. Eventually, a glorious cathedral was built in Saint Francis' name. As beautiful as it was, he never would have granted such extravagance. Clare could see how easily people were swayed into easing the restrictions. She did not want that for her convent. She continued her requests to the pope for a rule that followed the vision of Saint Francis. Clare was so convinced Francis' vision was the path to God that she would not accept any substitute.

There were many new religious groups forming in the thirteenth century. If the church did not recognize them officially, the group ran the risk of being labeled as heretics. They could be excommunicated and no longer able to receive the sacraments. Every time Clare sent a letter to the pope asking to follow a guideline different than other religious groups, she ran the risk of shutting herself and her sisters off from the church. The pope kept writing new rules to try to appease Clare but still provide for her convent in dire times. Each time Clare rejected the proposals. Eventually, she took it upon herself to write her own set of rules for papal approval. Finally, two days before her death in 1253, she received a papal bull granting her request. As she lay on her deathbed, she repeatedly kissed the paper granting her request. Now she knew Francis' vision would live on.

Reflection

There are not many people who have such a clear vision for their lives. So many kids go away to college and have no idea what they will major in let alone what they want to do for the rest of their lives. Clare had perfect reception for God's call to her. At eighteen she left home and began her calling that lasted forty-one years. I think in her solitude she was able to focus and easily define what was important to her. Trying to get through my day with all of its distractions, I get pulled in so many different directions. It is no wonder I have difficulty discerning God's plan.

I love Clare's persistence. She was a quiet woman who simply wanted to live the contemplative life offered in the Gospels. She whole heartedly believed God would provide for her, so there was no need to be concerned with temporal matters. The one worldly matter that was worth her focus was the privilege to live as Jesus commanded in the Gospels. In her situation most people would have simply lived under the rule that most closely fitted their ideals. Clare did this, but guided by her clear vision, she continually appealed to the pope for approval to live as she wanted.

There is a difference between being persistent and being stubborn. I corner the market on stubborn. One time I was on a business trip in Chicago, and the airport was closed due to weather. I didn't think it looked too bad, so I rented a car and started the five-hour trip home. After five hours in the car, but only fifty miles outside of Chicago, the highway patrol shut down the highway. I was lucky enough to get the last room in a dingy motel. I got home the next day four hours after the next flight out landed. I could have enjoyed a nice meal in Chicago, relaxed and come home the next day, but I knew better. I could beat the elements. Clare knew when it was important to take a stand and when it was important to let go and let God provide.

In 1958 Pope Pius XII named Clare the patron saint of television because one Christmas Eve Clare was too ill to attend Midnight Mass. She lay in her bed, but was able to see through the walls and see the entire Mass. After Mass the nuns came to her bedside and Clare described the little details of that celebration. It may be a bit of a stretch, but with many of the crazy shows that are on TV, it seems we need someone to intercede for us, and she has a connection as close as anyone.

Saint Clare's Chicken Saltimbocca Meal

Inspired Menu

The saltimbocca is a traditional dish from Italy, one that might have been served to Clare when she was a child. The bean accompaniment is a healthy dish that could be eaten as a main course with pasta and one that Clare might have made from food donated to her and the sisters. Almonds are an ingredient found in many Italian dishes. The dessert makes me think of the wonderful foods found in Assisi.

Saint Clare's Chicken Saltimbocca

Serves: 6

Prep time: 15–20 minutes

Cook time: 1 hour

Preheat oven: 350° F

You will need:

 1 ½ pounds chicken tenders pounded to ½-inch thickness (12 tenders)

 12 paper-thin slices proscuitto

 4 ounces provolone cheese sliced into 12 portions

 12 toothpicks

 salt and pepper to taste

 2 tablespoons olive oil

 1 sweet onion chopped (around 2 cups)

 4 carrots peeled and chopped into ½-inch coins (around 1½ cups)

 1 large red pepper sliced into ½-inch by 2-inch rectangles (around 1½ cups)

 1 teaspoon minced garlic

 8 ounces "baby bella" mushrooms, sliced

 1 (14.5-ounce) can diced tomatoes with basil and garlic

 optional garnish: fresh, chopped Italian parsley

Pound chicken tenders flat. Take each chicken tender and place enough proscuitto on top of the chicken to almost cover it. Then place a slice of provolone cheese on top. Taking the smaller side of the chicken, roll up the chicken and close with a toothpick. Season with salt and pepper. Repeat this until all of the tenders are rolled up.

Place a large skillet over high heat and add olive oil. Place the chicken in the skillet and quickly brown on all sides. Remove the chicken from the skillet and place into a 9 x 13-inch baking dish.

Using the skillet where the chicken was browned, sauté the onions and carrots for 5 minutes over medium-high heat. Lower the heat to medium and add the red pepper and garlic and sauté for another 5 minutes. Pour the onion mixture over the chicken. Sprinkle the mushrooms into the baking dish. Finally, pour the tomatoes over everything.

Bake for 30 minutes. Stir the vegetables and juices after 15 minutes and again before serving.

To serve, place two chicken rolls on a plate and top with vegetables and juices. Garnish with some chopped Italian parsley.

Poor Clare Beans
Serves: 6
Prep time: 5 minutes
Cook time: 25 minutes

You will need:

    3 cloves garlic, smashed

    2 tablespoons olive oil

    1 teaspoon crushed red pepper flakes (add more or less to taste)

    1/4 teaspoon freshly cracked black pepper

    1 cup chopped sweet onion

    2 bunches escarole, rinsed and torn

    1 (28-ounce) can whole peeled plum tomatoes

    1/2 teaspoon dried oregano

    1/2 teaspoon dried sweet basil

    1/4 teaspoon salt

    1 (19-ounce) can cannellini beans (white kidney beans), drained, but not rinsed

    optional garnish: fresh chopped flat-leaf parsley

In a 12-inch skillet sauté garlic, olive oil, red pepper flakes, black pepper and onions over medium-low heat for 15 minutes. Add escarole and sauté for 3 minutes. Add the juice from the can of tomatoes then crush the tomatoes in your hands and drop into the pan. Alternatively, you can place the tomatoes in a food processor and pulse for 1 minute, and then pour into the pan. Add oregano, basil, salt and beans and stir on medium-low heat for 5 minutes.

Saint Januarius Salad
Serves: 6
Prep time: 10 minutes
Cook time: 10 minutes

You will need:

    3 blood oranges, skinned and sliced into 1/2-inch rounds

1 cup balsamic vinegar

1/2 cup toasted pine nuts

Place oranges on a plate. In a small saucepan, reduce balsamic vinegar over medium-high heat to 1/2 cup. This should take 7–10 minutes. Let the vinegar cool and then drizzle over the oranges. Sprinkle with pine nuts.

Saint Januarius was a bishop in Naples in AD 305. Emperor Diocletian was a pagan and had Saint Januarius and some of his fellow Christians beheaded for their beliefs. For years the church has kept a vial of Saint Januarius's blood as a special relic. In the year 1389 someone noticed that the clotted blood had liquefied, then later clotted back into a solid. Several times a year the bishop of Naples holds a Mass in honor of Saint Januarius. The relic is present and the blood liquefies through the course of the Mass.

ALMOND TART

Serves: 10

Prep time: 10 minutes

Cook time: 30 minutes

Preheat oven. 325° F

Crust

You will need:

1 cup toasted slivered almonds

1 cup all-purpose flour

1/2 cup sugar

pinch of salt

1/2 cup (1 stick) unsalted butter, softened

1 teaspoon vanilla extract

Pulse almonds in a food processor for 10 to 15 seconds. Add flour and pulse another 10 seconds. Add sugar and salt and pulse for 10 seconds. Add butter and vanilla and pulse until fully blended (about 1 minute). Spread on the bottom and sides of an 11-inch tart pan. Bake for 15 minutes.

Filling

You will need:

> 1 (8-ounce) package softened cream cheese
>
> 2 eggs
>
> 1 cup powdered sugar
>
> 1/2 teaspoon almond extract

Place the cream cheese in a large bowl and mix on low until smooth. Add eggs one at a time. Mix on medium for 1–2 minutes. Add powdered sugar and almond extract and mix for 1 more minute. Pour filling into cooled crust. Bake for 25 minutes. The filling will be a dark golden brown and still jiggle a little. Remove from the oven and let cool.

Topping

You will need:

> 1/2 cup toasted slivered almonds

Garnish

You will need:

> 10 strawberries, tops removed

Slice the strawberry from the tip almost all the way through to the top, leaving about 1/8 inch still together. With your thumb and fingers, fan out the strawberry.

To serve, sprinkle tart with toasted slivered almonds and top with strawberry fan.

Dinner Conversation

Copy the following questions on pieces of paper and put them in a bowl and place on the table. While people are eating, pass the bowl around and have each person pull out a question. Everyone can take a turn answering the questions.

1. Could you give all you own to the poor and go be with God?
2. Why do you think it was so important for Saint Clare to press for the privilege of poverty?
3. What do you think God is calling you to do with your life? Are you doing it?
4. Can you discern when it is important to take action and when to let God provide?

Saint Clare's Meal Prayer

Prayer to Saint Clare

O wondrous blessed clarity of Clare!
In life she shone to a few;
after death she shines on the whole world!
On earth she was a clear light;
Now in heaven she is a brilliant sun.

O how great the vehemence of the
brilliance of this clarity!
On earth this light was indeed kept
within cloistered walls,
yet shed abroad its shining rays;
It was confined within a convent cell,
yet spread itself through the wide world.

—Pope Innocent IV

notes

saint elizabeth of hungary

PATRON SAINT OF:

Bakers,

Countesses,

Those Mourning the Death of a Child,

the Falsely Accused,

the Homeless,

Nurses,

Tertiaries,

Widows

and

Young Brides

Born: circa 1207

Died: November 17, 1231

FEAST DAY:

November 17

elizabeth: an unlikely servant

Saint Elizabeth was born a princess in an opulent castle in the northeastern corner of Hungary. Everything she wanted was at her disposal. As was the custom in the Middle Ages, her father, King Andrew II of Hungary, searched for a suitable husband for his daughter. Four years after her birth King Andrew determined his Elizabeth would marry Louis of Thuringia, Germany. Louis was eleven years old at the time and was slated to inherit the lands of Thuringia, Hesse and Palatinate.[1] Once the negotiations were finalized, Elizabeth was sent to meet her betrothed husband with a dowry of beautiful, expensive gifts. She and her attendant made the difficult journey through the mountains to the Wartburg, a spectacular castle precariously balanced on top of a cliff. Here Louis's mother, Sophia, raised Elizabeth and her betrothed side by side. Many hagiographers depict Sophia as the wicked step-mother in *Cinderella*. It makes for a good story, but it doesn't exactly ring true. Sophia was a pious woman who taught both Louis and Elizabeth important Christian values.

In 1221, after the two married, how they were raised became clear by the way they treated their subjects—with the same care and respect Sophia showed them. Elizabeth made it her practice to attend Mass regularly and pray devoutly. She gave food to the poor from special granaries set aside specifically for this reason. She also nursed the sick all while maintaining her duties of nobility. Elizabeth eventually had three beautiful children. Soon after each birth, she dressed herself as a peasant and climbed down the rocky mountainside to bring her babe to the church. There she placed the baby on the altar and offered it to God and begged him to receive it as his servant and to bless the child.[2] As Elizabeth grew in her faith, her prayer and almsgiving didn't seem to satisfy her desire to be close with God. She wanted to do more.

During the Middle Ages most nuns, priests and nobility had confessors assigned to be their spiritual guides. These confessors worked closely with an individual to help root out sin, which they accomplished on many fronts. The confessor questioned the individual on all aspects of his or her life and requested confessions whenever necessary. He observed the amount of almsgiving a person performed and made suggestions accordingly. He looked at the lives of the people with whom he was working and compared their lives to that of Jesus and suggested adjustments wherever necessary. Confessors were like personal trainers for the soul. Many of the nobility who consulted confessors would not even consider any actions without discussing them with their confessor first. Saint Elizabeth was no different in this regard. After she was married a few years, she sought out the strictest of confessors, Master Conrad of Marburg. Under his tutelage, she was even more zealous in her acts of piety. During a two-year famine, she fed the poor from her special granaries. When they were emptied, she opened up the special reserves for the castle and gave away all of the grains available. The castle cupboards were almost bare and then, after much prayer, the following year's crops were prolific.

Elizabeth was deeply concerned about the sick peasants of Thuringia. She spent much of her time nursing the ill. Typically, people came to the castle to personally ask for the special assistance they required. Elizabeth saw what a hardship this was for the ill to try to climb the mountain to beg for help. In response, she had a hospital built at the base of the mountain to care for all those who could not make the climb. She spent time in this hospital giving personal attention to the ailing. On one occasion she felt such compassion for a leper that she brought him to the castle and gave him her bed to sleep. There she nursed him until Louis came home from a crusade. Louis barely entered the castle before he was bombarded by the officers of his household. Quickly, they reported the atrocity they felt Elizabeth had committed. When Louis entered the room and saw the leper in his bed, he, like Elizabeth, could see Christ lying in his midst.

After six years of marriage, while Louis was on his way to the Holy Land in 1227, he died suddenly of tuberculosis. Elizabeth left the court and wandered. Some argue she was forced out of the court by Louis's brother, who took over the princedom, but many believe Elizabeth left the court by choice to become a tertiary, or layperson, in the third order of Saint Francis. She vowed a life of chastity and obedience as well as a life of service to others. Master Conrad seemed to focus on obedience as her path to God. He beat her with a rod if she dared question his recommendations. The marks lasted for weeks, and the lessons lasted longer. Elizabeth once commented:

> We are like the reeds growing on the bank of a swift flowing stream. When the waters rise they bow before them and the flood passes over without breaking them. But when the water recedes they rise up joyfully, full of strengthening sap. So must we bow our heads under the weight of humiliations that we may stand erect in joy and confidence.[3]

Soon after Louis's death Master Conrad convinced Elizabeth to renounce her children. Master Conrad believed "a mother's love for her children weakens the strength of her passion for the divine."[4] Next Master Conrad sent away Elizabeth's two closest companions. He believed that, without them, Elizabeth would only have God to cling to. Each thing he asked of Elizabeth was a test of her love for God. Each test Elizabeth accepted as her path and bowed her head to the will of Master Conrad. After years of excessive fasting and beatings, she died on November 17, 1231, at the young age of twenty-four.

REFLECTION

Living in the twenty-first century, I have a difficult time understanding some of the choices Elizabeth made. I can't imagine allowing someone to beat me in God's name. I believe life provides enough tribulations, and I don't need to have pain purposely added to it. I also can't imagine giving my children away as a means to get closer to God. I understand the concern that a mother would place her children before God in her heart. However, I believe when I watch over my children like a mother bear, I am taking care of the gifts God entrusted to me. Loving my children is not mutually exclusive to loving God. God resides in everyone—by loving people, we are loving God. In many ways I think Saint Elizabeth should be the patron saint for those who suffer from domestic violence, or anyone really, who is manipulated and brainwashed into believing she is not worthy of the life she is given. Elizabeth, for all of her love, warmth and care for others, had no one looking out for her best interests. Clearly, Master Conrad had his own agenda (and not Elizabeth's soul) when he sent her closest friends and children away. But that, I realize, is my enlightened twenty-first-century mind at work.

While I can't rationalize, explain or in any way pretend to understand Elizabeth's choices and suffering, I do still, in many ways, relate to her. Despite her own suffering, Saint Elizabeth could see Christ in everyone. She lived to make others happy and to serve others. I see women like Elizabeth everywhere I go—selflessly and quietly giving of themselves. For example, a good friend of mine works for pennies as a social worker trying to help the needs of others. She also is the mother of three children and does an amazing job teaching her children how to love and care for others. A few years ago she and her husband were invited to a wedding. They didn't have much money, so they

Many times Saint Elizabeth is pictured with a rose. This stems from a story about Elizabeth bringing bread to the poor during a severe famine. The castle had tapped into its special reserve of food and was quickly depleting its supply. Elizabeth couldn't bear to see others going hungry while she still had food to eat, so she sneaked into the pantry and carried loaves of bread under her cloak. Someone had seen her take the food and alerted her husband. As Elizabeth left the house, Louis approached her and demanded she open her cloak and give back the food. When Elizabeth did as she was told, she opened the cloak only to show a beautiful bouquet of red roses.

scrimped to save enough cash for the airfare to get to the wedding. My friend had about twenty dollars left to buy a dress. She found a cute one at a local resale shop. When she and her husband arrived at the wedding, one of the guests approached my friend and told her she should have worn a nicer dress to a wedding, and then walked away and wouldn't talk to my friend for the rest of the evening. This person could not see past my friend's dress to the incredible person she is. My friend does so many wonderful things for others, it is easy to find Christ in her actions. This person didn't take the time to see that. I know I have been guilty of the same thing on occasion. I might see someone with tattoos covering his body and immediately I think, "Oh no, this person is trouble." Then I find myself with a broken-down car and that same tattooed person, whom I judged unfairly before, is the only one who stops to help me. Saint Elizabeth gives me a wonderful reminder to take a deeper look at people and recognize that Christ lives in all of us.

Saint Elizabeth's "Hearty" German Bierocks Meal

Inspired Menu

Bierocks are pockets of bread with a meat filling and are a popular German-American delicacy, which take on a new meaning when associated with Saint Elizabeth. The bread reminds me of the bread that Saint Elizabeth so often gave to the needy, and the substantial meat filling reminds of me of the strong character Saint Elizabeth possessed inside. While the main course is German, the cucumber salad honors Elizabeth's ancestry, as it is a traditional Hungarian course. For dessert I have created a decadent ice cream sandwich based on the flavors of the Black Forest cake in honor of the time that Saint Elizabeth spent living in the Thuringian Forest in eastern Germany. The actual Black Forest is located in southwestern Germany, where for years people have been enjoying Black Forest cakes. This dessert gives a Thuringian spin (as in a Saint Elizabethan spin) on the original Black Forest cake.

SAINT ELIZABETH BREAD POCKETS (BIEROCKS)

Yields: 18 bierocks

Prep time: 25 minutes

Cook time: 30 minutes

Preheat oven: 350° F

Tip: Any extra bierocks can be frozen for up to 2 months.

You will need:

    1 (3-pound) bag frozen bread dough rolls, thawed to room temperature

    1 pound ground sirloin

    1/2 pound pork sausage

    1/2 teaspoon salt

    1/2 teaspoon ground black pepper

    1 cup chopped onion

    2 tablespoons mustard

    1 cup sauerkraut, rinsed and drained

    2 cups shredded gouda

    1 egg

    2 tablespoons sesame seeds

Season sirloin with salt and pepper then place it in a 10-inch skillet. Brown seasoned sirloin, sausage and onion over medium-high heat until it is cooked through. Remove the meat from the heat and drain the grease from the pan. Add mustard and sauerkraut and stir until evenly mixed. Let the meat mixture cool for 5 minutes. Add cheese and stir to distribute evenly. Roll out defrosted bread dough into 3-inch circles. Place 1/3 cup of the meat mixture on top of a circle. Place another dough circle on top of the meat. Pinch the edges together to enclose the filling. Repeat this until all of the rolls are completed. Brush beaten egg on top of each dough ball, and then sprinkle with sesame seeds. Bake for 20 minutes or until golden brown.

SKILLET APPLES

Serves: 6

Prep time: 15 minutes

Cook time: 40 minutes

You will need:

    3 Granny Smith apples, peeled and sliced

    3 Golden Delicious apples, peeled and sliced

    1 teaspoon ground cinnamon

    1/4 cup sugar

    1/4 cup brown sugar

    1/4 cup water

Place apples in a 10-inch skillet. Sprinkle with cinnamon, sugar and brown sugar. Pour water into the pan and cook over medium-low heat, covered for 35–40 minutes, until the apples are somewhat soft. Stir occasionally.

SAINT ELIZABETH OF HUNGARY'S CUCUMBER AND TOMATO SALAD

Serves: 6

Prep time: 15 minutes

Sitting time: 1 hour

Salad

You will need:

    2 large cucumbers, peeled, sliced and quartered

    2 1/2 cups tomatoes, seeded and chopped

Dressing

You will need:

    1/4 cup sour cream

    1/4 cup mayonnaise

    1/4 teaspoon dried oregano

¼ teaspoon minced garlic

1 teaspoon finely chopped chives

¾ teaspoon white vinegar

¼ teaspoon salt

pepper to taste

In a medium bowl combine sour cream, mayonnaise, oregano, garlic, chives, vinegar, salt and pepper. Place the dressing in the refrigerator for at least one hour (the taste improves if refrigerated overnight). When ready to serve, place the cucumbers and tomatoes in a bowl and spoon dressing over top. Stir until all of the tomatoes and cucumbers are covered.

SAINT ELIZABETH'S GERMAN BLACK FOREST ICE CREAM SANDWICHES

Yields: 12 sandwiches

Prep time: 30 minutes

Cook time: 12 minutes

Preheat oven: 350° F

Chocolate Cookies

You will need:

10 tablespoons butter or margarine, softened

½ cup granulated sugar

½ cup firmly packed brown sugar

1 teaspoon vanilla

1 egg

1¼ cups flour

½ cup cocoa powder

¾ teaspoon salt

1 teaspoon baking soda

1 cup mini semisweet chocolate chips

Filling

> 2 pints softened cherry cordial ice cream or substitute Ben and Jerry's Cherry Garcia ice cream. (If neither are available, use softened chocolate chip ice cream with 1/2 cup chopped maraschino cherries added.)

Cream butter and sugars together in a large bowl until fluffy. Add egg and vanilla and thoroughly mix together. In a separate bowl sift together flour, cocoa powder, salt and baking soda. Slowly mix in the flour mixture with the butter mixture. Stir in the chocolate chips. Place golf ball-sized dollops of cookie dough on a baking sheet and bake for 10–12 minutes. Let the cookies cool on a rack. When the cookies are completely cooled, scoop 2 to 3 tablespoons of ice cream on top of one cookie and then top with another cookie. Store in freezer until ready to serve. (If the ice cream is softened a little, it is easier to place onto the cookies.)

DINNER CONVERSATION

Copy the following questions on pieces of paper and put them in a bowl and place on the table. While people are eating, pass the bowl around and have each person pull out a question. Everyone can take a turn answering the questions.

1. What do you feel was Saint Elizabeth's best attribute?
2. Discuss Elizabeth's choices in life. Do you agree or disagree with them? Why?
3. What choice would you make differently from Saint Elizabeth and why?
4. What do you feel are your biggest obstacles to a relationship with God?
5. Have you seen God in someone and been surprised to find God there?

SAINT ELIZABETH'S MEAL PRAYER

Daily Prayer for the Workers at the Calcutta Orphanage

Dearest Lord, may I see you today and every day in the person of your sick, and, whilst nursing them, minister unto you.

Though you hide yourself behind the unattractive disguise of the irritable, the exacting, the unreasonable, may I still recognize you, and say: "Jesus, my patient, how sweet it is to serve you."

Lord, give me this seeing faith, then my work will never be monotonous. I will ever find joy in humoring the fancies and gratifying the wishes of all poor sufferers.

O beloved sick, how doubly dear you are to me, when you personify Christ; and what a privilege is mine to be allowed to tend you.

Sweetest Lord, make me appreciative of the dignity of my high vocation, and its many responsibilities. Never permit me to disgrace it by giving way to coldness, unkindness, or impatience.

And O God, while you are Jesus my patient, deign also me to be a patient Jesus, bearing with my faults, looking only to my intention, which is to love and serve you in the person of each one of your sick.

Lord, increase my faith, bless my efforts and work, now and for evermore, Amen.[5]

NOTES

[1] Elizabeth Whitehead, *Saints for the Married* (Liverpool: Mercier, 1949), p. 2.

[2] Whitehead, p. 7.

[3] Whitehead, p. 20.

[4] Anja Petrakopoulos, *Sanctity and Motherhood* (New York and London: Garland, 1995), p. 273.

[5] Veronica Zundel, *Eerdmans' Book of Famous Prayers* (Grand Rapids, Mich.: William B. Eerdmans, 1983), p. 99.

notes

saint notburga

saint notburga: making it right

The only information about Saint Notburga's life comes from a wooden plaque that decorates her tomb. This beautiful carving tells only the saintly details of her life. To understand her better, it is important to understand what life was like for a poor peasant girl in the mid-thirteenth century. Born into one of the poorest families, she was a slave to a lord and his manor. Her family was most likely given a small parcel of land, about half of an acre, on which they built their house, barn and garden. The barn was most likely attached to the house in order to keep the animals close and warm. There was no indoor plumbing, and the winters were treacherous. Life, to say the least, was extremely precarious. If the elements, nature, malnourishment or disease didn't get to the poor—taxes invariably did. However, there were some positive things about being a serf. A noble family father would often be out fighting a war or traveling to his other homes, but most serf families remained intact—the father was home to protect his family, and the mother was there to care for her young.

Saint Notburga's story begins in the Austrian Tirol, looking up at the Alps. When she turned eighteen, she began working for the lord of her manor, Count Henry Rattenberg. Here she could work in the relative warmth of a castle. Ottilia, the count's wife, put Notburga to work in the kitchen. Every day Notburga made an abundance of food and served any leftovers to the poor villagers begging outside the kitchen door. As long as the count's mother was alive, Notburga was allowed to do this. The count's mother was not yet cold in her grave when Ottilia commanded Notburga to stop feeding the poor and start feeding the pigs. All leftovers were now directed to the swine. Notburga did as she was told, but she would eat less herself and give her leftovers to the poor. After a while Notburga couldn't bear it any longer, and without regard to her own personal outcome, she again began the practice of giving all of the leftovers to the poor. As soon as Ottilia found out, she immediately fired Notburga.

Notburga had to leave the comfort of the castle and begin looking for work elsewhere. At harvest time she found a job with a local farmer. Just as she had at the castle, she worked very hard for the farmer. There is a wonderful legend told of her while she was working there. One beautiful Sunday morning during the harvest the church bells rang, calling people in for Mass. Notburga got up from the fields and headed for the church. The farmer yelled to her to come back. There were only a few good days to harvest and he needed every extra hand on such a gorgeous day. She was not deterred. She argued with the farmer and threw a sickle in the air yelling, "Let this decide." The sickle hung in the air like the first quarter moon, a sign of a good harvest.[1] With the sickle still hanging, I picture Notburga walking through fields of wheat, the sun shining in her long blond hair and her arms outstretched as she heads toward the church. I see the faces of the other serfs as they stare at the sickle and watch their friend Notburga head to Mass. It's quiet except for the song of the birds and the wind blowing the tassels on the wheat.

Back at the manor house the count felt his home had been swallowed up by his wife's spitefulness. All the bad that happened to him he attributed to his late wife, Ottilia. Eventually he remarried and asked Notburga to come back to the manor house and work for him, this time as a housekeeper. She was overjoyed to be back in the warmth and beauty of the castle. Without Ottilia there, she was free to do as she wished with the leftovers. It seemed that the count appreciated her presence in his home. When she was dying, she asked Count Henry to continue feeding the poor. He agreed.

REFLECTION

When I first heard this story, it reminded me of an old fairy tale in which good and evil are evenly pitted against each other. At first glance Ottilia seems so much like the wicked stepmother, and Saint Notburga like Cinderella herself. It is easier for me to view Ottilia as total evil and believe that I would act differently. Upon closer inspection, though, Ottilia may not be completely evil. What if she was merely considering that the pigs need to be fed to fatten them up for market? Fatter pigs equal more money. I'm sure she rationalized she was simply trying to make smart decisions for the estate. Her decisions remind me of a story I heard about a large corporation. As a perk, each employee was able to eat lunch for free in the company dining hall. For many years the company would take any leftovers and serve them to the poor. Some of the kitchen employees realized this and began making extra food to create more leftovers. Soon the company profits were declining and the company needed to find ways to cut back. The solution was to stop serving leftovers to the poor to encourage the kitchen employees to make less food. Less food waste equals more money for the company. These decision makers have a moral responsibility to feed the poor, but they also have a responsibility to the stockholders. It was the easy choice to simply stop giving away leftovers. They would have to have been much more creative to respond to both issues. I would hope that if I were in a similar situation, I would be able to think like the count's mother and find a way to serve the poor and the bottom line at the same time.

I admire Saint Notburga's conviction to do the right thing regardless of her personal consequences. Here she was working in the manor house with all its benefits, and she had the gumption to continue feeding the poor. She knew she would be fired and become the person begging for food. But she fed the poor anyway. It is very easy to look in hindsight and decipher right from wrong, but in the heat of it, it is not quite as simple. I love that it was simple for Saint Notburga. She kept God first always, so she was ready when she had to make the difficult decisions.

Each Advent I resolve that I will look for something nice to do for someone else and make sure to do it, even if it is a little inconvenient. If I see that someone's car needs a jump, I offer to help, even if it will make me late to my next task. If a young mother is trying to maneuver her stroller through the door, I run to open it for her. These are small things I should be doing anyway, but I think if I am not actively looking for them, I might miss them. My thought is that it will be easier to be ready for the difficult decisions when I routinely make good decisions on the easier choices. I believe Saint Notburga lived her life always making the right choices, both big and small.

NOTBURGA'S NOT-A-BURGER MEAL

Inspired Menu

When I was trying out this meal on my family, my children thought I chose pork for the main course because it was "not a burger." Actually, the pork in this meal reminds us that Saint Notburga gave the leftovers to people instead of pigs. Bread pudding is a dessert that can easily be put together with leftovers. A peasant would never want to waste any food, so this dessert celebrates her peasant upbringing.

Pork Tenderloin With Peach Basil Salsa

Serves: 6

Prep time: 5 minutes

Cook time: 20 minutes

Pork Tenderloin

You will need:

>   2¹/2 pounds pork tenderloin
>
>   ¹/2 cup packed brown sugar
>
>   1¹/2 teaspoons kosher salt
>
>   1 teaspoon dried ground chipotle pepper (spicy, adjust to taste)
>
>   1 clove garlic, finely chopped
>
>   2 tablespoons olive oil

Preheat outdoor grill. In a medium bowl mix brown sugar, salt, chipotle pepper, garlic and olive oil. Rub brown sugar mixture over the pork tenderloin, totally coating the meat. Cook directly over the flames for 2 minutes on each side to sear in the juices. Move the tenderloin to a part of the grill where the meat isn't over direct flames and cook for another 10–20 minutes. The pork will be ready when a meat thermometer placed in the center of the tenderloin reaches 145° F for medium doneness and 160° F for well done. Remove from the grill and let stand for 10 minutes before cutting.

Peach Basil Salsa

You will need:

>   2 cups thawed frozen or fresh peaches (If using frozen or unripe peaches, add 1 teaspoon brown sugar.)
>
>   1 tablespoon finely chopped basil
>
>   1 tablespoon chopped red onion
>
>   1 tablespoon finely chopped fresh jalapeno pepper (remove the seeds for a milder taste)

Chop peaches into ¹/2-inch cubes and place into a large bowl. Add basil, onion and jalapeno pepper. Stir to mix all items fully. Season with salt and pepper to taste.

To serve the pork, cut the tenderloin into ¹/2-inch slices. Place 2 or 3 slices onto each plate. Spoon salsa over the pork.

NOTBURGA'S TWICE-BAKED SWEET POTATOES

Serves: 6

Prep time: 25 minutes

Cook time: 1 hour 10 minutes

Preheat oven: 400° F

Time Saver: Make the potatoes ahead of time. Just save the second baking time for when your guests arrive. The potatoes can be frozen for up to 2 months. Simply thaw and then bake.

You will need:

    5 sweet potatoes (about 6 inches long)

    1 tablespoon butter

    1 Granny Smith apple, skinned and chopped into 1/2-inch cubes

    1 tablespoon cinnamon sugar

    2 tablespoons melted butter

    1/4 cup quick oats

    1/4 cup flour

    1/4 cup brown sugar

    1/4 cup chopped pecans (optional)

    1/4 cup honey

    1/4 teaspoon cinnamon

    scant 1/4 teaspoon allspice

Wash potatoes and pierce with a fork. Bake for 35–40 minutes. You will know the potatoes are ready when you can easily pierce them with a fork.

While the potatoes are cooking, take a medium saucepan and cook the butter, apple and cinnamon sugar over medium heat for 5–10 minutes. Make sure to stir regularly so the apples do not burn. The apples will be soft, but still firm when they are ready. Remove the apples from the heat and set aside until the potatoes are ready.

In a medium bowl, mix melted butter, oats, flour, brown sugar and pecans with a fork. Make sure to fully mix all of the ingredients together. It will be somewhat moist, but crumbly when ready. Set aside for later use.

When the potatoes have finished cooking, let them cool for 5 minutes. Cut the potatoes in half lengthwise. Gently scoop the potato from the skin. Try to leave a 1/4 inch of potato next to the skin to make a nice cup for the potato mixture. Don't worry if you rip some, you will only need 6 or 8 good potato cups. In a large bowl combine the meat of the potato with the apple mixture, honey, cinnamon and allspice. Evenly scoop this mixture into the potato cups you reserved. Top each of the potatoes with the oat mixture. Press it in a little so it doesn't all roll off. Place the potatoes in a 9 x 13-inch baking dish. Bake for 30 minutes.

SAUTÉED SPINACH
Serves: 6–8
Prep time: 5 minutes
Cook time: 18–20 minutes

You will need:

    1 tablespoon oil

    1 clove garlic, peeled and smashed

    2 bags fresh baby spinach

    3 tablespoons freshly grated Parmesan cheese

In a large skillet with high sides, heat oil and garlic over low heat for 10 minutes. Raise heat to medium-high and add one bag of spinach. Cook for 3 minutes until the spinach has cooked down. Add the remaining bag of spinach and cook for another 5 minutes. Make sure to turn the spinach while it is cooking. Serve the spinach on a plate and sprinkle with Parmesan cheese.

BREAD PUDDING WITH BOURBON SAUCE
Serves: 9–10
Prep time: 15 minutes
Cook time: 1 hour
Preheat oven: 350° F

Bread Pudding
You will need:

    1 (16-ounce) package cinnamon raisin bread

    1 tablespoon butter

    3 eggs

3 cups whole milk

1 teaspoon vanilla

½ cup sugar

Cut bread into ¾-inch cubes and place into a 2-quart buttered baking dish. In a large bowl beat eggs, milk, vanilla and sugar with mixer on a low speed for 1 minute. Pour the egg mixture over the bread and turn the bread gently, so all cubes are soaked. Let soak for 10 minutes. Place the 2-quart baking dish in a shallow pan of hot water and place in the oven and bake for 1 hour.

Bourbon Sauce

You will need:

½ cup (1 stick) butter

1 tablespoon bourbon

1 cup confectioner's sugar

½ cup whole milk

1 egg yolk

In a medium saucepan melt the butter over medium heat for 3 minutes. Add bourbon and confectioner's sugar. Whisk until fully combined. Whisk in milk then add egg yolk while rapidly whisking. Cook for 2 more minutes.

To serve, place a scoopful of pudding into a bowl and then drizzle with the bourbon sauce.

DINNER CONVERSATION

Copy the following questions on pieces of paper and put them in a bowl and place on the table. While people are eating, pass the bowl around and have each person pull out a question. Everyone can take a turn answering the questions.

1. Can you think of a time when you chose the easy thing instead of the right thing?

2. Do you think Notburga was able to show compassion for others because she was raised in a close family?

3. Would you be able to make the same decisions as Saint Notburga if you were in her place?

4. What are some things you can do to help other people?

Saint Notburga's Meal Prayer

Vindicate me, O Lord,

for I have walked in my integrity,

and I have trusted in the Lord without wavering.

Prove me, O Lord, and try me;

test my heart and mind.

For your steadfast love is before my eyes,

and I walk in faithfulness to you.

(Psalm 26:1–3)

Note

[1] Sarah Fawcett Thomas, et al., eds., *Butler's Lives of the Saints: November* (Collegeville, Minn.: Liturgical, 2000), p. 123.

notes

saint didacus of spain

PATRON SAINT OF:

Franciscan Brothers,

the Diocese of San Diego

and

Franciscan Laity

Born: circa 1400

Died: November 12, 1463

FEAST DAY:

November 13

didacus: the gentle gardener

Many of the medieval saints I highlight in this book were raised by someone other than their parents. It isn't surprising considering what a common custom this was for the nobility in medieval Europe. Noble daughters were often raised by their future in-laws or passed around to various noble homes to be instructed in the many areas a young lady must know. These young girls were taught how to sew, how to manage the properties while their husbands were gone and, most importantly, how to behave like proper women. Some noble children were given to abbeys along with a dowry. Many noble parents believed this "payment" of a child to an abbey (in place of a tithe) would ensure the parents' entry into heaven. Meanwhile, the girls were prepared for a life in the church, receiving basic instruction in reading and writing in their native tongue, the Psalter and all important church teachings. Boys learned the same as subjects as girls, but were also taught to read and write in Latin. All important documents of the time were written in Latin, and the priests and brothers required full access to that information.

As you might expect, peasants were not afforded the same opportunities as their noble counterparts. Therefore, most young peasant children stayed with their families and repeated the cycle of their ancestors. As a *villein*, or a peasant in the feudal class, Didacus's life offered very little in terms of education, wealth, opportunities or even health. In fact, life was often quite miserable for the poor, because many of the feudal lords in the area were tyrants. Feudal lords imposed unreasonable taxes and punished their villeins aggressively. Under a tyrant lord, the disparity between the riches of the lord and the poverty of his peasants was great. While feudal lords lived in (relatively speaking) lavish manors and had endless supplies of food (from the villeins), most villeins had difficulty paying their rents or keeping enough food to feed their own families. Faced with these limited options, many parents relinquished their children. Saint Didacus was no exception. When he was a young boy, his parents, hoping to offer Didacus a better chance at life, gave him to a hermit priest who lived in a cave high up on a hillside near the village where Didacus was born. What a difficult sacrifice Didacus's parents made, but what a wonderful opportunity for him.

Despite being separated from his parents, Didacus's life must have been idyllic in comparison to the peasants or even the townspeople's lives. Up on the hillside Saint Didacus worked side by side with the hermit priest under the glowing Spanish sun. Together they cultivated a garden of glorious vegetables that were plentiful enough to fill not only their own bellies, but those of the nearby poor. They also meticulously carved spoons out of wood and sold them at the market. They earned plenty of money to survive, and again, they had plenty left over to give to the poor. Their days were filled with prayer and meditation, all the while they could look out over the vast countryside below and drink in the beauty. They did not live in the city with rats and feces. They did not live on a manor with the fear of being beaten. Instead, they lived separately in their own private Garden of Eden.

After some years of this idyllic life, Didacus felt called to go back home and join a friary where he could help others. He began his calling as a lay brother, wearing the gray robes of the Observant Friars Minor. This group closely followed the ideals Saint Francis preached. Their mission, as commanded in Matthew, was (and still is) to "proclaim the good news: …Cure the sick, raise the dead, cleanse the lepers, cast out demons. You received without payment; give without payment" (10:7–8).

Soon after becoming a Franciscan, Didacus was sent to the Canary Islands. He quickly became adept at converting people during his four-year stay. After his mission ended, he moved back to Spain and lived in several different friaries.

In 1450 Didacus, along with a large group of friars, headed to Rome to attend the canonization of Bernardino of Siena, a saint from their order. On the trip to Rome, Saint Didacus was asked to accompany Father Alonso de Castro for the difficult journey—twelve hundred miles from Seville to Rome on foot. The trip started out on a high note. They were very excited to go to Rome and celebrate one of their own attaining sainthood. As they reached Rome, Father de Castro fell ill and Didacus had to care for him. Didacus stayed by the father's side and compassionately nursed him back to health. His superiors noticed the empathy and care he held for Father de Castro, so they asked him to stay on at the convent of Ara Caeli in Rome and help with the increasing number of sick friars. Without any medical training (he wasn't even able to read) Didacus obeyed his orders and began his life in medicine—caring for the ill. His life with the hermit, no doubt, prepared him for this new obligation.

Didacus had learned all about the medicinal herbs in the hermit's Spanish garden, and he was familiar with their healing properties. While serving the sick, he ministered the proper herbs and salves and sat by his patients' bedsides and prayed and meditated until the patients could feel the calm that he himself felt in his Spanish hillside garden. After three months, the infirmary substantially cleared out and Didacus traveled back to Spain. There he lived out the rest of his days serving the poor in the friaries of Salcedo and Alcala in Castile. He died on November 12, 1463.

Didacus lived a peaceful and unassuming life, and he would have remained unknown forever had it not been for a special miracle attributed to him in which he saved the life of Don Carlos, son of King Phillip of Spain. Don Carlos fell down several steps and received a severe head wound. Engulfed with infection, his head was so swollen he lost his sight. The great doctors from the famed medical university in Alcala consulted with the royal physician on Don Carlos's case. Try as they might, the top minds couldn't cure the ailing prince. Determined to save his son from certain death, King Phillip and his entourage marched to the Monastery of Jesus Maria and had Didacus's body exhumed. The holy remains were carefully moved to the room of Don Carlos. The muslin wrapped around Didacus's head was slowly removed and gently placed on Don Carlos's injured head. The young prince drifted off into a sweet dream where he met and spoke with Didacus. Don Carlos showed immediate signs of improvement. Each day the swelling in his head reduced, and his sight gradually returned. The king saw this miracle as proof that Didacus was a saint, so he petitioned Rome to have him canonized.[1] On July 2, 1588, Didacus was officially pronounced a saint.

> Saint Didacus is the Latin form of San Diego. In the early 1600s when Spain was at the height of its glory, a Spanish ship, the *San Diego*, landed in San Miguel Bay, California. Shortly after the ship landed, the crew held Mass on November 12, Saint Didacus's feast day, and named the spot in his honor.[2]

REFLECTION

I love the core philosophy of the Franciscans, which is to help others and to give without receiving repayment. I believe Saint Didacus's parents taught their son this ideal by giving him to the hermit priest to be raised. I can't imagine the courage it takes to offer a child to another to give him or her a chance at a better life. There are countless young women today who make this same sacrifice for their children, when they give them up for adoption so that another family can love and care for their children in a way they could not possibly do on their own.

Saint Didacus was able to give others the gifts his parents gave him. With his soft, gentle manner he cared for patients compassionately. He gave to them and expected nothing in return. It takes a special person to nurse the ill. When my father-in-law had Alzheimer's disease and had to go into a nursing home, I was so touched by the care my mother-in-law and some of the nurses provided. The disease had made him angry and hard to deal with. Some of the nurses wanted nothing to do with him, but others could see past the disease. These nurses took time with him despite his anger. They gently tended to his needs and watched the subtle signs of his disease as it progressed. While they took care of his nursing needs, my mother-in-law spent hours with him giving him all of the love and comfort he deserved. It took a team of people to care for him, and the nurses took a lot of the grunt work so that my mother-in-law could spend hours praying with my father-in-law, feeding him and holding his hand much the same way Saint Didacus cared for the ill centuries ago.

When I look at the life of Saint Didacus, it is his individual acts of compassion toward others that add up to great virtue. He made choices every day to positively affect someone else's life. The nurses at the nursing home make those same choices on a daily basis. I know they aren't getting paid commensurate to their contributions, yet they still come in each day smiling and take the time to help someone other than themselves. It was difficult for my mother-in-law to see her husband in such pain. It would have been much easier for her to leave everything to the professionals and go on with her life. But she didn't. She made the choice every day to go in and positively affect her husband's life. Although Saint Didacus is not the official patron saint for hospital workers or caregivers, I can picture his calm presence guiding these caregivers in their godly work, and I often think of him and call on him throughout my own day in the midst of caring for others.

plant a saint didacus garden

Saint Didacus spent many of his first years as a hermit communing with God while out in his garden. Take the time to plant a garden in his honor. If you have room, make a spot for yourself in the garden where you can enjoy the beautiful plants and the scents they offer. Sit and meditate in the early mornings.

I would suggest dividing the garden into two sections. One section for herbs and another for vegetables. All of these things will require a lot of sunlight. Many of the recipes in this book call for basil, rosemary, sage and thyme, so I would suggest planting those in the herb section. For the vegetable section I would consider planting Roma tomatoes, sweet peas and zucchini. My sister-in-law is a fantastic gardener and can make anything flourish; I, on the other hand, am not blessed with a green thumb. I have, however, been able to grow the vegetables and all of the herbs mentioned above. It is very inexpensive to start these from seed, but for me, it is easier to make a stop at my local nursery and buy the plants already started. If you have enough space, plant a little extra. Donate the extra vegetables you harvest to a local food bank.

Saint Didacus's Spanish Garden Meal

Inspired Menu

This hearty vegetarian meal utilizes some of the flavors of Spain while still celebrating the wonderful vegetables that might have been found on Saint Didacus's hillside garden.

Saint Didacus's Toasted Spanish Eggplant Slices

Servings: 6

Prep time: 15 minutes

Cook time: 20 minutes

Preheat oven: 350° F

Tip: To speed up this preparation, make the flour coating ahead of time and store in a jar or container until you are ready to use it.

You will need:

 1 1/2 pounds eggplant (2 small to medium eggplants)

 salt

 1 cup flour

 1 teaspoon garlic salt

 3/4 teaspoon onion powder

 3/4 teaspoon ground cumin

 1/4 teaspoon ground chipotle pepper

 1/2 teaspoon ground black pepper

 3 beaten eggs

 2 cups vegetable shortening, or as needed

Remove the skin from the eggplant and then slice into 1/4-inch disks. Sprinkle generously with salt and place into a colander and set aside for 15-20 minutes. In a large flat bowl mix flour, garlic salt, onion powder, cumin, chipotle and black pepper. Set this aside.

Place the beaten eggs in a separate bowl.

Take the eggplant slices and rinse them off with water and then immediately pat dry. Take the dry eggplant slices and dredge in the flour mixture. Next, cover the eggplant with beaten egg. Let any excess egg drip off of the eggplant and dip into the flour mixture one final time. Repeat until all slices are covered.

Place the shortening in a large pot over medium-high heat. When the shortening looks hot, test it by dropping a little of the flour into it. The shortening is ready when the flour sizzles and rises to the top. Place the eggplant in the shortening and cook for about 2 minutes on each side. You may place as many pieces that fit in the pan without touching. They will be golden brown when ready. Remove and place on a paper towel until all of the eggplant is cooked. You may need to add extra oil during this process.

Baked Tomato Salsa

Serves: 6

Prep time: 5 minutes

Cook time: 30 minutes

Preheat oven: 350° F

You will need:

>   24 ounces of cherry tomatoes, halved
>   1 teaspoon olive oil
>   1 tablespoon finely chopped fresh jalapeno pepper
>   2 tablespoons finely chopped red onion
>   salt to taste

Place cherry tomato halves into a large bowl. Drizzle with olive oil. Add jalapeno pepper and red onion and top with salt and pepper to taste. Gently toss the tomatoes to cover with the onions and jalapeno peppers. Pour into the bottom of a 9 x 13-inch baking dish.

Place the tomatoes cut side up and then sprinkle with salt. Bake in a 350° oven for 30 minutes.

FETTUCCINI WITH ALFREDO SAUCE

Serves: 6

Prep time: 5 minutes

Cook time: 15 minutes

18 ounces refrigerated fettuccini

2 tablespoons unsalted butter

1 bunch green onions (about ¼ cup), chopped

2½ teaspoons minced fresh garlic

1 teaspoon salt

2 tablespoons all-purpose flour

2½ cups heavy cream (you may substitute half-and-half)

½ teaspoon dried oregano

½ cup grated Parmesano-Reggiano cheese

Place butter, onions, garlic and salt in a large saucepan over medium-high heat. Stir the mixture until the onions soften. Sprinkle the flour into the pan and stir for 2-3 minutes. Make sure all of the flour is coated with butter. Slowly add the heavy cream, stirring constantly. Add the oregano and Parmesano-Reggiano cheese and continue stirring over medium-high heat for about 5 minutes until the sauce thickens. (Do *not* let the sauce come to a boil or it will curdle.)

Boil the fettuccini according to the directions on the package.

To serve, twirl the fettuccini on a plate and top with the Alfredo sauce.

BANANAS DIEGO

Serves: 6

Prep time: 5 minutes

Cook time: 4 minutes

3 tablespoons unsalted butter

4 bananas sliced into 1/2-inch coins

1 teaspoon ground cinnamon

2/3 cup honey

3 tablespoons Sambuca liqueur

vanilla ice cream

Place honey in a bowl and mix with Sambuca. Set this mixture aside for later. Place butter and bananas in a 12-inch skillet over medium heat. Stir until all of the butter is melted. Sprinkle with cinnamon and then add honey mixture. Cook for another 3 minutes.

To serve, place one large scoop of vanilla ice cream in a bowl then pour 1/6 of the banana mixture over the ice cream. Repeat for remaining servings. Serve immediately.

Dinner Conversation

Copy the following questions on pieces of paper and put them in a bowl and place on the table. While people are eating, pass the bowl around and have each person pull out a question. Everyone can take a turn answering the questions.

1. Can you think of ways you can show compassion for another?
2. Is there a place you go to be alone with God and pray?
3. To which side of Saint Didacus do you most relate? His side of meditating in the garden or his side of caring for others?
4. Can you think of times that you preach Jesus' word?

Saint Didacus's Meal Prayer

A Reading From the Gospel According to Matthew:

> Then the righteous will answer him, "Lord, when was it that we saw you hungry and gave you food, or thirsty and gave you something to drink? And when was it that we saw you a stranger and welcomed you, or naked and gave you clothing? And when was it that we saw you sick or in prison and visited you?" And the king will answer them, "Truly I tell you, just as you did it to one of the least of these who are members of my family, you did it to me."

—*Matthew 25:37–40*

Notes

[1] William H. Prescott, *History of the Reign of Philip the Second King of Spain, Vol. II* (Philadelphia: J.B. Lippencott, 1882), pp. 466–470.

[2] *The Journal of San Diego History,* available at www.sandiegohistory.org

[3] Gaynell Bordes Cronin and Jack Rathschmidt, *The Blessing Candles* (Cincinnati: St. Anthony Messenger, 1997), p. 81.

notes

saint josephine bakhita

PATRON SAINT OF:

Sudan

Born: circa 1868

Died: February 8, 1947

FEAST DAY:

February 8

josephine bakhita: the "forgiving" one

In 1877 on a typical afternoon in Darfur, Sudan, Bakhita and her good friend were playing just outside their village. Their giggling obscured the sound of two knife-wielding men, who slowly crept up on the eight-year-old girls. One of the men ordered Bakhita to go fetch something from behind a bush and told her friend to continue on her way. Startled, Bakhita did as she was told. As soon as she was hidden from view, the men grabbed Bakhita, covered her mouth and carried her away. She was forced into a small hut that didn't show the light of day. After an agonizing month, she was pulled out to begin her way to the slave market. Outside once again, Bakhita was free to feel the hot sun soak into her bones and the gentle breeze caress her skin. She spent the next several days marching through Africa while the men gathered more villagers to become slaves. The journey was difficult. The slaves were not fed much and were whipped at whim. At her first opportunity, Bakhita escaped with another young girl. They ran to the nearest village and approached the first person they encountered. Bakhita relayed her story and asked for help. Instead of helping her, the man helped himself by selling her to another slave trader. After another long, painful journey, she was sold at the slave market.

Bakhita had a series of owners. At the first owner's home she was beaten so badly that she took a month to recover. She was soon sold to a Turkish general and was a personal maid to the general's wife and mother. The two women were extremely intolerant and whipped their slaves for the slightest infractions. Along with various other demands, the ladies wanted to brand their slaves with special tattoos to mark their property. One day while the general's wife and mother looked on, Bakhita and a fellow slave were branded. First Bakhita turned her head to watch as the tattoo artist drew the designs on her friend's ebony skin. Bakhita lay in silence while the artist made cut after cut deep into her friend's flesh. Finally her friend passed out from the pain. It must have been horrific for Bakhita to know what was coming next. In one long session, the tattoo artist carved more than sixty tattoos all over

Bakhita's body. It took her nearly two months to recover from this atrocity. After long years of enduring abuse at the hands of the women, Bakhita was sold so her masters could move back to Turkey.

Callisto Leganini, an Italian consul, first met Bakhita when she served him at the Turkish household. He was immediately drawn to her inner spirit and made arrangements to purchase Bakhita. For the first time since she was a young child, Bakhita was treated with respect, and once again she was able to enjoy moments of peace and tranquility.[1] Callisto was called back to Italy, and Bakhita asked if she could go with him. He had intended to release her from the bonds of slavery, but Sudan was at war and the two had to make a quick escape out of Africa. Good thing they did, because many of the slaves were captured during the fighting and resold to new owners. Together with Callisto's friend, Augusto Michieli, they safely landed in Italy. Augusto's wife greeted them at the harbor, and upon seeing the slaves she hinted and cajoled until finally Callisto acquiesced and sold Bakhita to the family.

Bakhita went with the Michieli family and worked as a loving nanny to their daughter Mimmina. For eight years Bakhita nurtured Mimmina as if she was her own daughter. Bakhita must have enjoyed all of the hours in the nursery softly humming old African melodies to rock Mimmina to sleep. Eventually the Michielis opened a hotel in Africa and were ready to move back there to settle in. Because Mrs. Michieli didn't want to subject her daughter to the unrest in Africa, she petitioned the Canossian sisters in Venice to grant permission for Mimmina and Bakhita to live in the catechumenate. After considerable debate, the request was granted, and once again Bakhita found herself living in a new home. The Canossian sisters taught Bakhita about the Catholic faith and helped her define the feelings she had always felt deep inside her but couldn't name. During her stay in the convent she reflected:

> [The sisters] helped me know God, Whom I had experienced in my heart since childhood, without realizing Who He was. I remembered how as a child, I had contemplated the sun, the moon, the stars, and all the beautiful things of nature, asking myself who could be the master of it all! And how I had felt a keen desire to see Him, know Him, and pay Him homage. Now, at last, I knew Him…![2]

Now for the first time since she was a young child, she felt a sense of belonging. After the Michieli family was settled into Sudan, they came back to Italy to retrieve the girls. As much as Bakhita liked the family, she was ready to be baptized and take the steps to become a Canossian sister. When Bakhita informed Mrs. Michieli of her desire to stay in Italy, Mrs. Michieli rejected the idea. Bakhita found her voice and held firm. With the backing of the Canossian sisters and the cardinal patriarch, Mrs. Michieli was informed that slavery was illegal in Italy; therefore, Bakhita was free and within her rights to stay at the convent.

Bakhita took the vows of the Canossian sisters and the name Sister Josephine Bakhita. The sisters at the convent were very active in helping others through apostolic work, but Bakhita was needed for the more mundane jobs. She cooked and cleaned, embroidered and greeted people at the door of the school. She performed all of her tasks with love and care and consideration for others. Bakhita recognized that she could do God's will in any task. She didn't have to wait for the perfect scenario to help others. As she neared the end of her life, she couldn't walk and required a wheelchair to get around. The bishop approached Bakhita and asked her what she did while sitting in her wheelchair. Bakhita replied, "What do I do? Exactly what you are doing—the will of God."[3] Her patience and presence of mind to fully comprehend that even in difficult or mundane situations you can still be doing the will of God is insightful.

Bakhita means "fortunate one." When Bakhita was first captured, she was stunned into silence. The kidnappers prodded her to reveal her name, but no words came. Finally one of the captors said, "Fine, we will call you Bakhita! That's what we will call you! Bakhita means 'the lucky one' and you are lucky indeed."[4]

REFLECTION

I have spent a lot of time watching other people do many wonderful things to help others. Nuns like the Canossian sisters care for the poor. Firefighters will put their lives in danger to help save the life of a stranger. Some doctors travel to impoverished countries to help people who could never pay back the gift the doctors present. When I compare my life to the life of these people, I begin to feel very inadequate. Until I read that quote from Josephine Bakhita, it never occurred to me that maybe God is not looking for me to do one great thing. Maybe what God wants from me is to say yes to his little invitations to help others throughout the day.

Bakhita's willingness to accept her position in life was a result of her capacity to forgive. When asked if she could excuse those who caused her so much suffering, she replied, "I pity them! No doubt they were unaware of the anguish they caused me. [T]hey did not know what they were doing."[5] Her ability to forgive echoes Jesus on the cross when he said, "Father, forgive them; for they do not know what they are doing" (Luke 23:34).

I am amazed at the depth of her ability to forgive. Most people would understand if Bakhita let anger monopolize her thoughts. Instead she chose to forgive, freeing her thoughts to contemplate all of the wonderful things life has to offer. Saint Josephine Bakhita is an anomaly. For most people it is not so easy to forgive someone's transgressions. I read an article about a serial rapist during the sentencing phase of his trial. Before the final sentence was passed down, the judge asked if any of the victims would like to speak. One of the women approached the rapist, looked him directly in the eye and said, "You did not break me. You did not steal my joy. I forgive you."[6] She was able to get on with her life. She married, had children and, most importantly, joy in her life. The article didn't mention anything about the other women. I can only wonder if they were able to get past the terrible ordeal they had to endure. Were they able to open themselves again to joy in their lives? It took tremendous courage and strength for the woman to be able to forgive a transgression as horrible as rape, just as it took Bakhita to forgive her abusers. By taking that scary, difficult step of forgiveness, both the woman and Bakhita did as Jesus commands, "[F]orgive your brother or sister from your heart"(Matthew 18:35).

The document for the canonization process attributed a medical healing to Saint Josephine Bakhita as confirmation of her presence in heaven. In 1939 Sister Angela Mari Silla fell ill with terrible knee pain. She was diagnosed with arthritis synovitis, a condition in which the lining of the joint fills with a painful fluid. For ten years Sister Angela Mari endured the pain until she could bear it no longer. The doctors were all in agreement that the nun required surgery to remove her kneecap. On the morning of October 12, 1947, six months after Bakhita's death, Sister Angela Mari was scheduled for surgery. That very same morning she was miraculously healed. She could walk again because the pain and swelling was gone. Several non-medical people testified to this miracle as well as her doctors. The sisters believed that Sister Angela Mari was healed through the intersession of Saint Josephine Bakhita.[7]

SAINT JOSEPHINE BAKHITA'S BEEF AND POTATOES MEAL

Inspired Menu

This menu is traditional Sudanese food that Saint Josephine Bakhita may have eaten as a child or prepared when she was older. My friend Mabrouka Kuku Tiya moved to the United States from Sudan about seven years ago, and she was kind enough to show me this traditional Sudanese cooking. The dessert is not Sudanese; however, it is a very forgiving dessert to make. Most baking requires precise measurements and exact timing for the recipe to turn out correctly. The most difficult part of this dessert is whipping the cream. If you are nervous about that, you could always substitute with a whipped topping alternative. (Make sure it is thawed before folding it in.) So to remember Josephine Bakhita's ability to forgive, I like this forgiving dessert.

SAINT JOSEPHINE BAKHITA'S SUDANESE GROUND BEEF AND POTATOES

Serves: 6

Prep time: 30 minutes

Cook time: 60 minutes

You will need:

1/2 pound ground beef

3/4 teaspoon salt

2 cups water

1/4 teaspoon cinnamon

2 tablespoons tomato sauce

1 small clove garlic, minced

6 russet potatoes, skinned and diced (8 cups, 1/2-inch cubes)

1/2 cup canola oil

1 teaspoon salt

4 carrots, skinned and chopped (1 cup, 1/2-inch coins)

1/4 cup green pepper, chopped

Smash ground beef and salt into a 5-quart soup pot and cover with water. Boil meat over high heat for about 20 minutes until all the water has boiled away. Stir occasionally. Stir in cinnamon, tomato sauce and garlic and remove from heat. Put oil in a 3-quart saucepan over medium-high heat. Add half of the potatoes and cook for 20 minutes, stirring occasionally. The potatoes will be soft and a little browned when ready. Place the cooked potatoes in the pot with the meat while cooking the remainder of the potatoes. When the rest of the potatoes finish cooking, add in with the meat. Cook the carrots in the remaining oil over medium-high heat for 4 minutes. Add the cooked carrots in with the meat and potatoes and stir all together until fully combined. Cook the green peppers in the skillet for about 3 minutes over medium-high heat. Add the green pepper in with the potato mixture and fully combine.

FuFu (Cornmeal Mush)
Serves: 6
Prep time: 2 minutes
Cook time: 4 minutes

You will need:

 4 cups water
 1 cup white cornmeal
 ¼ cup all-purpose flour

In a 3-quart saucepan bring water to a hard boil. Add half of the cornmeal and stir in with a wooden spoon. (About one minute of stirring.) If any lumps form, press them against the side of the pan with your spoon. Once the cornmeal has been mixed, add in the remaining cornmeal and stir in the same way. Stir for about 1 more minute. Then stir in the flour for 1 minute. Let the FuFu cook for 2 more minutes, stirring occasionally.

Beef Jerky Gravy
Serves: 6
Prep time: 15 minutes
Cook time: 30 minutes

You will need:

 4 tablespoons canola oil
 1 large sweet onion, chopped
 4 fresh okras, cleaned and sliced into ½-inch rounds
 2 ounces beef jerky
 2¼ cups water
 ¼ teaspoon cinnamon
 ½ teaspoon salt
 ¼ cup tomato sauce
 1 large clove minced garlic
 ¼ teaspoon cornstarch

Pour canola oil into a 3-quart saucepan along with onions and caramelize over medium-high heat for 10 minutes. Remove onions from the saucepan and set aside. Cook the okras for 4–5 minutes over medium-high heat until the vegetables soften and then set aside for later use. Place the beef jerky in a food processor and pulse for 3 minutes until the meat is pulverized. Add the onions to the food processor and pulse for 2 seconds to mix with the meat and chop the onions a little. Put the meat and onions into the saucepan with the remaining oil and stir. Add water to the saucepan and turn the heat to medium-high. Add cinnamon and salt and boil covered for 15 minutes. Then add tomato sauce and garlic and remove the lid. Turn heat down to medium low and cook for another 15 minutes. Add cornstarch and okras and stir until sauce thickens. Serve this over top of the FuFu.

COLLARD GREENS
Serves: 6–8
Prep time: 5 minutes
Cook time: 45 minutes

You will need:
    3 cups water
    3/4 teaspoon salt
    1 small sweet onion, chopped
    3 smashed cloves garlic
    1½ pound ham hock
    1 (1-pound) bag collard greens
    1 tablespoon malt vinegar

Place water, salt, onion, garlic, ham hocks and collard greens into a large covered stock pot over medium heat. Cook for 45 minutes until the greens are tender. Stir occasionally so the greens do not stick to the bottom. When greens are finished cooking, add vinegar to the pot and stir.

Forgiving Trifle

Serves: 9

Prep time: 15 minutes

You will need:

- 1 pound frozen pound cake
- ¼ cup almond-flavored liqueur (such as Amaretto)
- 1½ cups chocolate covered toffee bits (such as Heath bar)
- 1 (3.9-ounce) box instant chocolate fudge pudding mix
- 1 teaspoon coffee granules
- 2 cups whole milk
- 1 cup heavy cream

Cube pound cake into 1-inch pieces and spread across the bottom of a 2-quart dish to form a single layer. You will have a little cake left over. Drizzle cake with almond liqueur and then sprinkle with half of the toffee bits. Pour the pudding mix and coffee granules in a large mixing bowl. Add milk and mix the beaters for 2 minutes. In a separate mixing bowl, pour heavy cream and beat with clean beaters until stiff peaks form. Take a third of the whipped cream and stir it into the pudding mixture. Gently fold in the rest of the whipped cream. Only fold it in about 10–12 turns. The mixture will look somewhat streaked. Pour the pudding over the cake and toffee bits. Sprinkle the remaining toffee bits over the pudding. Refrigerate until ready to serve.

This is best when made a few hours ahead of time. It will keep overnight, but the toffee bits will soften with age.

Dinner Conversation

Copy the following questions on pieces of paper and put them in a bowl and place on the table. While people are eating, pass the bowl around and have each person pull out a question. Everyone can take a turn answering the questions.

1. Josephine Bakhita sat in her wheelchair and proclaimed that she was doing the will of God. Do you think you are doing the will of God right now in your life?
2. Is there anyone in your life you are having difficulty forgiving?
3. Would you be able to forgive someone for raping you or abusing you the way Josephine Bakhita was abused?

4. Would you be able to forgive someone if they hurt someone you love?

5. Josephine Bakhita has said that divine providence led her to God. Can you think of a time when you have felt the intervention of divine providence?

Saint Josephine Bakhita Meal Prayer

Josephine Bakhita wrote this prayer for the pronouncement of her religious vows.

Oh dear Lord, how good You are!

Could I but fly to Africa and proclaim aloud

to all my people

Your goodness to me!

How many souls would hear my voice

and turn to you.

Grant, O Lord, that they too, may know and love you![8]

Notes

[1] Maria Luisa Dagnino, *Bakhita Tells Her Story*, Loretta Hall, ed. (Rome: General House, Canossian Daughters of Charity, 1992), p. 22.

[2] Dagnino, p. 24.

[3] Dagnino, p. 53.

[4] Dagnino, p. 14.

[5] Dagnino, p. 29.

[6] Dan Horn, "'I forgive you, she says to rapist,'" *The Cincinnati Enquirer*, May 16, 2007, pp. A1, A12.

[7] Dagnino, pp. 67–69.

[8] Dagnino, p. 40.

notes

topical index

recipe index

patron saints index

table of equivalencies

1 teaspoon = $^1/_3$ tablespoon
1 tablespoon = 3 teaspoons
2 tablespoons = 1 ounce
8 tablespoons = 4 ounces or $^1/_2$ cup
1 cup = 8 ounces
2 cups = 16 ounces or 1 pint
1 quart = 4 cups or 2 pints
1 gallon = 4 quarts